MW00898430

GODWAY
DEVOTIONALS

PURSUING GOD ON THE WAY TO YOUR DREAMS

KATIE HOMER

ISBN 978-1-63575-003-4 (Paperback)
ISBN 978-1-63575-004-1 (Digital)

Christian Faith Publishing, Inc.
296 Chestnut Street
Meadville, PA 16335
www.christianfaithpublishing.com

Printed in the United States of America

God brought us into the arts. Let's bring them back to Him.

CONTENTS

DEDICATION

I dedicate this book to my uncle, George Franks, for his generous support and in loving memory of my cousin, Danny Goedken, and my aunt, Barbara Bond.

DAY 1

SPEAK YOUR HEART

Many times we expect people to read our minds. If they loved me, they should automatically know what I desire and what I need. I shouldn't have to communicate it to them—how unromantic is that?

But the reality is, no one can read your mind, except God. Not even Satan. So in order to get your needs met or have a dream fulfilled, it's often necessary to communicate your desires, rather than sit around and hope for them.

First, communicate your desires to God. Yes, He already knows what you need, but He wants you to be aware of what you need and to deliberately ask Him for it. We may think God is far too bothered to deal with petty requests. This would be true if God wasn't a personal God. But the truth is, He is deeply invested in every detail about your life. Engaging in dialogue with Him demonstrates your reliance and faith.

> "You do not have, because you do not ask God"
> (James 4:2 NIV).

9

"So I say to you: Ask and it will be given to you; seek and you will find; knock and the door will be opened to you" (Luke 11:9 NIV).

"If any of you seeks wisdom, you should ask God, who gives generously to all without finding fault, and it shall be given to him" (James 1:5 NIV).

Second, we must communicate our desires to others. Last weekend was the final show of my first big musical. It was always my dream to have both parents in the audience. I was just going to let it go until a friend of mine encouraged me to speak up. Both parents and my sister came, and a lifelong dream of mine was fulfilled!

"If you then, though you are evil, know how to give good gifts to your children, how much more will your Father in heaven give the Holy Spirit to those who ask him" (Luke 11:13 NIV)!

How many things do we not receive because we simply do not ask? May we not only strive to follow our hearts, but to make them known.

ask.

DAY 2

DON'T MISS THE POINT

This post is extremely personal for me. Consider it a confession.

I think often times we become so obsessed with one detail we miss the big picture. We become so consumed with one exercise that we miss the whole course.

For me this was fasting. While fasting is a good discipline, it became my religion. Rather than focusing on worship, prayer, scripture, or anything else, I thought that if I was fasting, I was being spiritually pleasing to God; and if I was eating, I wasn't.

In a nutshell, fasting became my God, and as it works with most extremes, overindulgence became my other god.

Then one night, it hit me.

Katie, you're missing the whole point! A relationship with God is not about food or lack of food. It's about a loving, imperfect, passionate, messy, and authentic union with your Creator. Fasting might be one of many channels, but it's certainly not a substitute.

> "And don't be concerned about what to eat and what to drink. Don't worry about such things. These things dominate the thoughts of

unbelievers all over the world, but your <u>Father</u>
already knows your needs. Seek the Kingdom of
God above all else, and he will give you everything
you need" (Luke 12:29–31 NIV).

"For the kingdom of God is not a matter of food
and drink, but of <u>righteousness</u>, <u>peace</u>, and joy
<u>in the Holy Spirit</u>; <u>whoever serves Christ in this
way is pleasing to God and</u> approved by others"
(Romans 14:17–18 NIV).

Performers, don't become obsessed with the weight on the
scale, with the height of your leg, the number of lines you have,
how much a job pays, how many likes you get on Facebook, or what
others think. Don't idolize your figure, your peers, the celebrity actor,
popular teacher, or the famous choreographer.

Remember why you do this—to feed your heart, to feel alive, to
bring joy to a broken world, to lift up others, give the hurting a voice.
<u>Love</u>, my friends. *That* is the point. It *must* start there, and the
rest will take care of itself.

Approach all your <u>classes</u>, <u>auditions</u>, and performances with
that purpose, and God will open doors to you no man can shut!

"Behold I have set before thee an open door, and
no man can shut it" (Revelation 3:8 KJV).

[handwritten:] The point is love
God will open doors no man
can shut.

DAY 3

LOOK AGAIN

Many times we have an image in our heads of what that perfect job or person should be like. We pass up many opportunities along the way because they do not match what we imagined. They are not important enough, big enough, attractive enough, worth our time, or going anywhere.

Well, that's what many people did with Jesus. They pictured a person of wealth, status, power, and obvious influence. What they got was a person who was the complete opposite in every way. For this reason, many missed out on a relationship with the Son of God. And they still are today.

God loves to disguise treasures to test our hearts. Satan loves to parade around as a wolf in sheep's clothing.

Thus, don't always let your first impression be your guide. What is pleasing to the eyes and to the ego can never satisfy. Put your energy toward those things that are pleasing to the heart. We must train ourselves to see as God sees.

> "So the last will be first, and the first will be last"
> (Matthew 20:16 NIV).

Ladies, don't assume the cutest guy at the bar will make you the happiest. In fact, he can make your life miserable. Pastor Steven Furtick says, "Women don't look for a body type. God's one for you will be unusual but proportional."

You want success in your life? Go after the humble things. The good-hearted things. For those are the places you will find God, who alone has the power to take you beyond your wildest dreams.

Go after the humble
good hearted things
there you will find
God.

what God opens no man can shut.

DAY 4

SUCH GREAT HEIGHTS

In order to become the best version of yourself—who God created you to be—you must surround yourself with the right people. This goes for friendships, spouses, and all other types of relationships.

It's amazing how much the attitudes and words around us affect our faith, motivation, and joy. Don't spend time with people who remind you how hard and unrealistic your dreams are. Stay in the company of those who remind you how big your God is and how much they believe in you.

Surround yourself with people who make you feel like your dreams are too small, not too big! People who love you in your lowest state and celebrate you in your highest. People who will ride the bus with you, before you ever get to the limo. God has blessed me with many of those people. You know who you are. Thank you.

In a spouse—find the one who makes your heart leap, not one who keeps your feet on the ground. If you want to take bold risks for God and allow Him to really use you, you must be with someone who shares that desire. This person must be more motivated by love than by fear.

In a friend—invest in those who see the good in everything and everyone. Those who lessen your burdens rather than adding to them. Pay attention to how you feel *after* spending time with them. You should feel joyful and reenergized, not drained and deflated.

A God-honoring relationship of any kind has no room for gossip, deceit, or negativity. Of course, you can—and should—authentically express your struggles and concerns. Just make sure a vast majority of your relationship is spent in gratitude, encouraging one another, talking about your dreams, and reminding each other how wonderful life can be.

> "Let no corrupting talk come out of your mouths, but only such as is good for building up, as fits the occasion, that it may give grace to those who hear" (Ephesians 4:29 ESV).

Let's continue to build each other up, standing on each other's shoulders, shooting for the stars, heads in the clouds, until we reach Heaven together.

let your words give GRACE to those who hear

DAY 5

MIRROR, MIRROR

This year, I received the best Valentine's Day gift ever. My friend hosted the first annual Women's Healing Event through her organization Peace Again. While I thought I would be doing *her* a favor by helping, it really was the biggest blessing to *me*.

One of the speakers led a workshop on emotional healing. Since it was Valentine's Day, she also gave us a few dating tips:

Many girls talk about how hard it is to find a good guy in NYC, especially since everyone seems to be so focused on their careers and unwilling to commit.

She said before she met her husband, she always attracted noncommittal men. Whenever she saw a cute guy, she would automatically turn away. Part of this stemmed from witnessing her parents' dysfunctional marriage.

Eventually, she realized that when you point the finger at someone else, three fingers point back at you. The issues you notice in others are a mirror for your own issues. In other words, you attract the kind of qualities you're subconsciously sending out.

She couldn't trust men because she couldn't trust herself. She couldn't find men who could commit because she could not commit.

She could not find who she was looking for because she hadn't yet found herself.

Rather than focusing on her love life, she needed to focus on loving life.

So she took a whole summer to date herself, eating at all her favorite restaurants, doing her favorite activities, and really falling madly in love with who she is as a person. She also began hanging out with healthy, godly couples who gave her a new picture of marriage, one built on mutual love and respect.

When the right man did come along, the goal was no longer to get him to like her. The goal was to be clear about who she was, invite him to come along for the ride and love all parts of her (even if he didn't "like" all of them), or else be fine moving on. His response? A marriage proposal.

Her main message was that in order to receive love, you must first create a vessel to hold that love. The right person won't have to fill an already full cup—they'll overflow it.

When you love who you see in the mirror, your love life will reflect that.

DAY 6

AVAILABILITY, NOT ABILITY

Last spring, I auditioned for a musical called *Hats Off to Liza*. I remember the audition like it was yesterday. I have always been a dancer first, but this was a singer's call. Not only would I be singing, but in a big room full of amazing singers who were also auditioning.

"Katie," I said to myself, "You either give 100 percent or none at all. That's the only way to do it."

The whole audition, even though I was terrified, I tried to hang on to my values and be kind to the other ladies in the room. I did my best to be friendly, strike up conversations, and focus on making them feel comfortable and reassured. I also pushed myself beyond my comfort zone and belted notes I didn't know I had in me.

After singing, dancing, tapping, and singing some more . . . there was only another guy and me left in the room . . . and we both booked the job! I will never forget the joy of that moment.

But the internal battle didn't stop there.

Throughout the rehearsal process, my self-doubt reared its ugly head several times as I doubted my abilities. I was clearly the weakest singer, and I didn't want to hold back the show and be the reason it did not do well. I even considered bowing out of the show a couple times, thinking that was the self-sacrificial, selfless thing to do.

After receiving encouragement from a few godly friends in the business and my incredibly supportive director, Lawrence J. Capici, I decided to rise to the occasion. Eventually, my confidence and faith in God and myself grew, and I ended up having one of the most amazing, life-giving, artistically-fulfilling, and well-received experiences of my entire life.

It's amazing what God can do when you put self-doubt and feelings of inadequacy aside and accept the mission He has called you to—whatever it is. I am learning that God is not in the business of handing out superpowers but of revealing what He's already put inside you. He does not call the prepared; He prepares the called.

As Pastor Nicky Gumbel puts it, God is not concerned with your ability, but with your availability. All you must dare to pray is, "Here I am, Lord. Send me."

DAY 7

A DIFFERENT WAY TO PRAY

Often times we think of prayer as a specific activity—quiet contemplation, meditating, fasting, being at church, and reading scriptures. But what if instead we began to see every activity as a type of prayer?

My doorman today talked about having to put his twenty-one-year-old cat to sleep. He was obviously very sad about it. Just being able to look him in the eye and tell him how sorry I was and share in his pain in that moment was such a powerful form of intercession.

Before, I would have zoned out, feeling a burden to fast, dedicate a Rosary to him, light a candle *later* during my "prayer time"—all good and decent things. But the gift of being fully *present* with someone, sharing a piece of your life and time with them, and listening to their heart is sometimes the most powerful form of prayer we can offer.

> "No, this is the kind of fasting I want: free those who are wrongly imprisoned; lighten the burden of those who work for you. Let the oppressed go free, and remove the chains that bind people" (Isaiah 58:6 NLT).

One weekend, I participated in a women's holding circle. You get a partner, and without saying a word, you just place your hands on their shoulders, hold them in your arms, or whatever you feel comfortable doing.

For about fifteen minutes of a guided meditation, you send them prayers and positive energies, letting them know they are safe and accepted exactly for who they are.

It was so incredibly moving, and I thought I was going to burst wide open because of the overflow of emotion pouring from my heart, eyes, and nose. Though we were silent, my partner said she felt like I was psychic because of the ways we interacted. Another person I was thinking of during the meditation sent me an email right afterward. This person lives in another country.

Don't limit God and prayers to a certain place, position, or posture. Prayer can be an act of service, a listening ear, a word of encouragement, a thoughtful gift, or a physical touch. This type of prayer makes God more tangible in a world that so desperately needs to feel the humanity of Christ.

As a popular African Proverb says, "When you pray, move your feet."

DAY 8

WHAT'S WORKING?

One day, I was sitting at McDonalds. There was a TV playing the news, stories complaining about politics, weather, etc. One man nearby mentioned that Americans are never satisfied. If they aren't complaining about one thing, it's another.

I know a lot of people who choose not to watch the news because it's so depressing. There is far too much emphasis on what's going wrong instead of what's going right.

What if the news channels focused on celebrating the good things in the world? What if politicians focused on encouraging one another, building each other up, and working together to make this country the best it can be?

> "Let all bitterness and wrath and anger and clamor and slander be put away from you, along with all malice. Be kind to one another, tenderhearted, forgiving one another, as God in Christ forgave you" (Ephesians 4:31–32 KJV).

I once attended a "Life Coaching Workshop" that touched on this principle in our own lives. The speaker said emotions are simply "symptoms" of our thoughts. They are not who we are, simply what we're experiencing. Therefore, by changing our thoughts, we can change our symptoms.

> "Whatever is true, whatever is honorable, whatever is just, whatever is pure, whatever is lovely, whatever is commendable, if there is any excellence, if there is anything worthy of praise, think about these things" (Philippians 4:8 ESV).

One of the ladies kept replaying and reliving the traumatic events in her life—like many of us often do—so she continued to live victimized, tormented, and powerless. The speaker encouraged her to instead focus on things that did work to get her out of the situation and things that could work in the future from preventing it from happening again.

Exerting negative energy further depletes your energy, putting you in a deficit. Exerting positive energy generates more energy, putting you in a surplus. Let's make sure the energy we're putting out is generating the greatest return of investment in our lives.

> "A joyful heart is good medicine, but a crushed spirit dries up the bones" (Proverbs 17:22 ESV).

So ask yourself . . . What's working in your life? What's going well? What are you grateful for? Simply focusing on that list will make it grow.

No matter what is or isn't working in our lives, God is always working. There's a reason the cross looks like a plus symbol. He is the Master of turning the negatives to positives; He *added* to our lives even though His was taken away.

May God continue to guard your spirits with truth, goodness, and love.

DAY 9

READY OR NOT

"When I'm in shape, I'll start auditioning."

"When I overcome this sin, I'll start going to church."

"When I figure out my career, I'll focus on relationships.'

"When I have more time, I'll pray more."

We spend so much time waiting for the right conditions, we end up *blocking* the right conditions:

— Auditioning will help you get in shape.
— Going to church will help you overcome that sin.
— Focusing on relationships with help put your career in perspective.
— Praying more will clear out the clutter in your life.

We are afraid to make a wrong decision and call it "putting God first." We have become passive and lazy in our pursuit and called it "trusting in God." We make excuses and call it "waiting on God."

But God is waiting on *us* to act!

Some of us are caught in a never-ending game of Hide & Seek. We are closing our eyes and counting, thinking that God is hiding from us and trying to make it as hard as possible to find Him.

It's time we stop counting, and start adamantly searching, leaving no stone left unturned.

As Pastor Rick Warren says, "God can only steer a car in motion."

Many people only focus on the part of free will that leads us to sin. They forget that free will is also one of God's greatest gifts, inviting us to participate in determining the course of our lives.

God's will is less about *what* you do than *how* and *why* you're doing it.

No more lazy, timid Christianity! It's time to make our own decisions, own them, and honor God in every single one.

> "For God hath not given us the spirit of fear;
> but of power, and of love, and of a sound mind"
> (2 Timothy 1:7 KJV).

DAY 10

MASTERPIECE

Most of us see God as a rigid scorekeeper who is most pleased with us when we are robotically and solemnly performing a religious exercise. As if our prayers matter more to him at 8:00 a.m. or when we're on our knees than when we're enjoying a concert or delicious food.

This couldn't be further from the truth! God is pro-pleasure! He is pro-passion! He is pro-dance-your-heart-out-laugh-til-your-sides-hurt-love-someone-so-much-you-can-hardly-breathe!

As a parent, which would bring you more joy—seeing your child bowing formally at your feet or observing them delight in a gift you've given them or a develop a passion they've discovered? Seeing them come alive would bring so much joy to your soul. A joyful child says a lot about the parent.

"The glory of God is man fully alive"
(Saint Irenaeus).

I love that quote! We serve an incredibly passionate God, and we are made in his image. Fully enjoying God's gift of life is the greatest gift we can give Him in return.

"Eternal Beauty! You act as if You could not live without Your creation, even though You are Life itself, and everything has its life from You and nothing can live without You. Why then are you so mad? Because you have fallen madly in love with what You have made" (St. Catherine of Siena)!

Before I quit my job in advertising to pursue a dance career, I felt a lot of guilt. Surely this was just selfish pursuit and not the self-sacrificing path God chose and required of me. So I spent a lot of time in fearful discernment.

"Why am I afraid to dance, I who love music and rhythm and grace and song and laughter? Why am I afraid to live, I who love life and the beauty of flesh and living colors of the earth and sky and sea? Why am I afraid to love, I who love love" (Eugene O'Neill's play "The Great God Brown")?

But once I took the plunge and started to live as my true self, my character, confidence, and relationship with God and others grew exponentially. When you are so filled up, you can't help but overflow onto those around you. That's why it's not only a privilege to pursue your passions, but your responsibility.

"Do not ask what the world needs. Ask what makes you come alive, because what the world needs are those who have become alive" (Howard Thurman).

I can honestly say that every single day since that decision has been incredible. No, not every day is perfect, but every day has purpose. It's the most liberating, energizing feeling in the world, and I can't imagine living any other way.

"Be who God meant you to be, and you will set the world on fire" (St. Catherine of Siena).

DAY 11

CHANGE YOUR MIND

Many of us struggle to find the balance between legalism and authenticity on our faith journeys. We follow rules simply to please God, instead of realizing that *we* actually benefit more from them.

God is so profoundly invested in our happiness, His boundaries are not for His own pleasure, but for ours. We focus so much on the short-term, instant benefits we're giving up and too little on the greater, lasting benefits His guidelines grant us.

Many of us think "repentance" simply means to be sorry. In actuality, the Greek word for "repent" is "metanoeo," which literally means, "to change your mind."

Once we begin to see God's laws more as "how-to tips" for our own happiness and protection, our relationship with God and sin changes drastically.

For example, no sex before marriage is not God's way of testing our faithfulness and discipline. It is His way of ensuring the deepest joy, pleasure, and intimacy and protects us from objectification, infidelity, and divorce.

"Flee from sexual immorality. Every other sin a person commits is outside the body, but the sexually immoral person sins against his own body" (1 Corinthians 6:18 ESV).

God doesn't say sexual immorality sins against Him; He said it sins against *us*.

When we realize this profound truth, we are able to live out our faith genuinely and gratefully, realizing that our struggle with sin is largely the result of not having all the information.

Furthermore, human beings by nature are more prone to self-preservation rather than obedience. So once we stop looking at the *what* and start understanding the *why*, our natural instincts kick in. Thus, our natural human tendencies could work for us instead of against us. How cool is that?!

"Do not conform to the pattern of this world, but be transformed by the renewing of your mind. Then you will be able to test and approve what God's will is—his good, pleasing and perfect will" (Romans 12:2 NIV).

So how do we do this? Simply ask God for wisdom and divine revelation in every area, and He will give it to you:

"If any of you lacks wisdom, you should ask God, who gives generously to all without finding fault, and it will be given to you" (James 1:5 ESV).

DAY 12

PURPOSE IN PAIN

You know that secret you have? The one you're ashamed about and pray no one finds out about? *That* is your biggest testimony and life's mission.

God never wastes a hurt. His specialty is bringing good out of bad situations. Whether you've been the victim of rape, bigotry, discrimination, sexism, objectification, or whatever it may be, you must see the bigger purpose and use your pain to help minimize the pain of others.

> "And we know that in all things God works for the good of those who love him, who have been called according to his purpose" (Romans 8:28 ESV).

They always ask why God lets bad things happen to good people. I believe it is because good people are the ones who are brave and determined enough to do something about it.

For example, I just watched a documentary on Netflix called *Brave Miss World*. It's about Miss Israel Linor Abargil who was crowned the winner of the 1998 Miss World competition, six weeks after being stabbed and raped.

It is certainly no coincidence that the victim of such a horrendous crime was exalted to a position of power and influence that enabled her to raise awareness of rape and help countless victims all over the world. Had this never happened to her, she would have been a swimsuit model. Now, she is a devout Jew, human rights lawyer, and activist.

> "I think many people who experience trauma end up working the same field to heal themselves. I turned this disadvantage into an advantage so that I could help other girls. They can see my face here instead of someone else. I think that would have helped me if I was in their shoes" (Miss Israel Linor Abargil).

Linor also explains the importance religion has played in her healing and recovery: "Before we find religion, we are always in trouble. Because we are always looking for something. And when we find it, which is God, we are no longer in trouble, because it is something stronger than us."

So if you're going through a hard time in your life, don't run from it—embrace it. Give your pain to God, and trade it for His immeasurable joy and blessings. Your life and so many others' lives depend on it.

DAY 13

PLEASURE THRESHOLD

We're familiar with the pain threshold—the point at which a person starts to feel pain. But we often forget to examine the pleasure that got us there.

You may remember from college economics, the Law of Diminishing Return. After a certain point, the rewards you get from something lessen the longer you consume it. In other words, it is possible to have too much of a good thing.

First, let's be clear that God is *pro-pleasure*:

> "So I recommend having fun, because there is nothing better for people in this world than to eat, drink, and enjoy life. That way they will experience some happiness along with all the hard work God gives them under the sun" (Ecclesiastes 8:15 NLT). Preach! Hallelujah!

But God is also *anti-excess*:

33

"Do not be with heavy drinkers of wine, or with gluttonous eaters of meat; For the heavy drinker and the glutton will come to poverty, and drowsiness will clothe one with rags" (Proverbs 23:20–21 NASB).

"If you have found honey, eat only enough for you, lest you have your fill of it and vomit it" (Proverbs 25:16 ESV).

A friend just sent me a truly enlightening article that talks about the trouble our culture has enjoying something pleasurable without going to extremes:

Nowadays, when we detect something is pleasurable, we tend to want to have our fill of it, to be completely sated with it. So if we like to ski, we become "avid skiers," or if we like tennis, we become "tennis addicts." If a man enjoys kissing his sweetheart, it's a given that he will sleep with her.

The Christian approach to pleasure is to delight in it for the moment, and then forget about it. What a blessing it is to be able to enjoy the little tastes of joy in life, seeing in them a small whisper of the joy of heaven, without having to be a slave to them, even in a small way. In other words, the real Christian can be satisfied with little pleasures, whether in food, or drink, or a goodnight kiss, or even the joy of friendship, without insisting on having more, more, more" (Rev. Thomas G. Morrow).

I *highly,* encourage you to read the entire article here: http://www.cfalive.com/resources/book-previews/christian-courtship/

The longings of our souls can never be filled by tangible things, so when we attempt to fill them insufficiently, it leads to even more emptiness and pain.

As hinted at above, we must be mindful of this in our artistic endeavors as well. In the pursuit of our dreams, we often lose sight of other aspects of life, equally or even more important to our personal fulfillment. No success, no matter how great, can take the place of quality relationships, spirituality, traveling, and life experiences.

This is also a danger living in New York City. With so much excitement and entertainment around us, it's easy to get caught up in the hustle and bustle of consumption and over-stimulation to where we become desensitized to the things that matter most.

So what are some steps we can take to combat this tendency?

- Savor a brownie one bite at a time and then move on to the next activity rather than the next helping.
- Hold your significant other in your arms, affectionately and presently, without letting it explode into a full-on make-out session.
- At a party, sip on a cocktail or two, allowing yourself to experience the high of great conversation, contagious music, and exhilarating dancing.
- Devote a couple hours to your craft each day, and then get lunch with a friend, get involved with your church, call your mom, plan a trip.

The irony? When you control your pleasures, you actually enjoy them more than when they control you.

Let this be our prayer:

> "Don't make me either rich or poor; just give me enough food for each day. If I have too much, I might reject you and say, 'I don't know the Lord.' If I am poor, I might steal and disgrace the name of my God" (Proverbs 30:8–9 NCV).

DAY 14

DON'T FALL. DIVE!

We always talk about falling in love, falling into a career, falling into an addiction. Falling by the nature of physics puts us at the mercy of gravity—an unchangeable force that brings us down.

Using our discernment and the power of choice, we need to consciously decide what is worth taking a risk for and then actively dive into what God is calling us to, not fall. Unlike gravity, God's unchangeable force is one that lifts us up.

Often times, we feel enslaved to those things we just kind of "fell into." A job. A relationship. An addiction. These are things in our life that seem to have lacked our desire or deliberate pursuit. In other words, they don't make us happy.

In high school, I fell into advertising. In college, I fell into an abusive relationship. In New York, I fell into an eating disorder. During each of these things, I felt as if I had fallen and couldn't get up. As if my lack of control getting into those situations meant a I was powerless to get out of them.

So let's stop living a mindless, passive existence, allowing life to just happen to us, falling from one thing to the next. Crawl out of whatever hole you're in, and walk bravely to the edge of your comfort zone. Then dive into God's world. Dive into God's love. Dive into God's will for your life.

"I can do all things through Christ who strengthens me" (Philippians 4:13 NKJV).

— You know that guy who treats you with kindness, respect, and acceptance, who loves you just the way you are and encourages you in your dreams . . . maybe he's not what you pictured in your head, but you know what, he'll be better. *Dive* into a God-honoring relationship with him instead of *falling* in love with the handsome jerk in the bar.

— You know that passion you always wanted to pursue but put it aside for a practical career out of duty, maturity, the desire to please everyone else, and the attempt to "grow up." Yes, the one that may not always pay your heating bill but sets your heart on fire. *Dive* into that passion instead of *falling* into another day job. God's provision will come, and in more ways than one.

— You know that alcohol addiction you fell into along the way of unmet desires, disappointments, loneliness, shattered hopes, unfulfilled dreams, depression, and debt? The one that's bringing more of those undesirable things into your life? Get up, Sister. Rise up, Brother. It's time to crawl out of that hole of despair and *dive* into a life of true substance instead of *falling* for a substitute. Experience the love and ecstasy of a God who will intoxicate your mind, body, and soul beyond your wildest imagination.

DAY 15

WHAT'S YOUR QUESTION?

Have you ever been at a crossroads in your life, where you had absolutely no idea what to do? No matter how hard you prayed, how many people you talked to, sermons you listened too, articles you Googled, or cookies you ate, you seemed to get further and further away from the answer.

Friends, I have a confession. I can write all the GODWAY devotionals in the world and post insights on my wall, but when it comes to figuring out the decisions in my own life, I have an awfully hard time.

The past week, I have been agonizing over a decision. Should my loyalties be to this person or this person? Is this decision unfair to person A? What about the feelings of person B? Wait, what about what makes *me* happy?

After three agonizing, sleepless days of this on repeat, I realized something. My main concern should not be with pleasing others or myself, but pleasing God. I had been asking all the wrong questions so I was getting all the wrong answers, or blocking them all together!

Here's what I felt God saying to me one night:

"Katie, do you really believe that what I say is true and necessary for your most abundant life? Then stop asking what makes him happy, her happy, or even yourself happy. Ask what makes *me* happy, and base your decision off that. Then all those other people will be happy too. You only fail to hear the right answer because you fail to ask the right question."

— Instead of asking do I love this person or this person more, ask which person makes me more in love with God.

— Instead of asking should I take this job or this job, ask which will produce the most fruits for the Lord.

— Instead of asking should I live here or there, ask God which will allow you to be a bigger witness for the Kingdom.

To put it another way, I think getting answers from God is much like a game of Jeopardy. The answers are already there in the Bible, sermons, and godly counsel. You just need to figure out the right questions to stay in the game.

DAY 16

WHAT'S THE DIFFERENCE?

As Christians, we like to talk a lot about how "different" we are. We're "different" from those selfish colleagues at work, we're "different" from those people that watch trashy TV shows, we're "different" from those promiscuous people at the club.

While our intentions may be honorable, this "different" mentality can subconsciously lead to pride, exclusivity, and alienation from others. Hence, we lessen the influence we are intending to have.

What makes us Christian is not that we are any less broken than others, but simply that we are more aware of our brokenness and need of a Savior. Many Christians act as if they need God's grace less than others, which contradicts the very essence of our faith.

> "The church is a hospital for sinners, not a museum for saints" (Abigail Van Buren).

How much more effective would Christianity be if we focused instead on how we're the *same*?

For example, which of these scenarios do you think is more effective in sharing God's love and transforming a person's life . . .?

So you're struggling with a drug addiction? Don't you know that your body is a temple of the Holy Spirit? I will be praying for you.

B. So you're struggling with a drug addiction? I struggle with a food addiction, so I totally understand you. I want you to know I'm here for you if you ever need to talk.

If we truly wish to be countercultural—in a world that focuses on our religious, political, cultural, and sexual differences—we must remember that God loves us all the *same*, and we are called to do likewise.

> "To the weak I became weak, to win the weak. I have become all things to all people so that by all possible means I might save some" (1 Corinthians 9:22 NIV).

People shouldn't know you're a Christian because you look, act, or sound like one, but because you *love* like one.

May the biggest difference we have be the difference we make.

DAY 17

NOTHING BUT THE TRUTH

If I could share one secret about living a joyful, peaceful life, it's this: *always, always, always* be honest with yourself and with others, in your career, dating, and relationships.

Our culture preaches a watered-down version of the truth. It tells us to be shrewd at work, savvy in business, and slick in our relationships. It sees flat-out honesty as "impractical," "inconvenient," and "immature."

It says things like:

— "Don't lay all your cards out at once."
— "You don't owe anyone an explanation."
— "That's for you to know. No one else."
— "Be smart about it."
— "They'll never know the difference."
— "Lighten up. Don't be so hard on yourself."

Have you ever been convicted in your spirit about something, but others discouraged you from acting on it in the name of prudence? For example . . .

— You don't feel right about a costume your director asks you to wear, but you're afraid speaking up will cost you the role.

— You don't feel right about dating two people at once, but you're afraid that being honest will make you lose both of them.

— You don't have peace about taking a certain position, but expressing any doubts might leave you unemployed.

But no matter how hard you try to put these thoughts aside, you feel that unrelenting pang of guilt and incongruence in your soul. It's like you're stuck in a prison of fear, held hostage by other people's opinions, values, and voices in your head.

> Jesus says, "And you will know the truth, and the truth will set you free" (John 8:32 NIV).

Friends, let me encourage you . . . *stop* living as a modified, watered-down version of yourself. *Stop* living by other people's rules and suffering under the weight of your own conscience.

Whenever I have followed my own inner compass, thrown caution to the wind, and spoke my heart, it has always worked in my favor and opened more doors than any half-truth ever could. There's nothing more liberating in this entire world that being your honest and authentic self and being accepted for it. *I pray you would experience that!*

> "Therefore, having put away falsetto, let each one of you speak the truth with his neighbor, for we are members one of another" (Ephesians 4:25 ESV).

If someone can't handle your truth, then they don't have to be a part of your life. But *you* have to feel good about you. No

43

opportunity, relationship, or feeling is as precious as being right with your own soul.

***A note on relationships . . . I firmly believe that any relationship, however platonic, should start from a place of openness and integrity.

> "The righteous man walks in his integrity; His children are blessed after him" (Proverbs 20:7 NKJV).

Pastor Rick Warren says, "Love is based on trust; and trust is based on truth. If you can't tell me the truth, I can't trust you. And if I can't trust you, I can't love you."

Guys, if you lie to a girl that you're dating. You're going to lie to your wife later on. The same goes for girls.

In a court of law, we're asked: "Do you solemnly swear that you will tell the truth, the whole truth, and nothing but the truth, so help you God?"

I challenge you to make this oath to God in every area of your life, and trust Him to be your defender and make good on His promise to provide you with the very best.

May you experience the freedom that comes from living out your truth. For in truth, that's the only way to truly live.

DAY 18

PERFECTION PARALYSIS

We put so much pressure on ourselves to be perfect and avoid mistakes—in our careers, relationships, and faith—that we end up inadvertently slowing down our own growth and maturity.

The paradox of perfection is the more determined we are to obtain it, the further we get from it. When we value perfection over growth, we allow it to shrink us. Our fear of failure blocks our success.

I can't tell you how many times I've hesitated, procrastinated, lost sleep, or been completely paralyzed because I was terrified of making the wrong decision. Recently, I began realizing that wisdom does not only come from our wise decisions, but our unwise decisions as well.

Taking the wrong job can motivate us to find the right job. Dating the wrong person can help us better recognize the right person. Going against your conscience can strengthen your convictions in that area. Falling out of a triple pirouette fifty times can lead to a flawless performance. Working through a conflict in a friendship can lead to a lifelong relationship.

The perfect illustration of this is our relationship with God. The times I've felt the most broken, helpless, confused, unworthy—

and anything but perfect—are the times I've developed a deeper level of intimacy with God.

Of course, I do not advocate being reckless in your decisions, indifferent to the outcome. But as long as our intentions are honorable and we're doing the best with the knowledge we have, we should not beat ourselves up but rely on God's grace.

> "Trust in the Lord with all your heart. Lean not on your own understanding. Seek His will in all you do, and he will show you which path to take" (Proverbs 3:5–6 ESV).

Another big danger in perfectionism is the "all or nothing" approach. We either become self-righteous and legalistic in our pursuit or wonder what the point is of even trying.

That's why society-induced perfection is the cause of everything from prejudice, discrimination, and arrogance to anorexia, suicide, and depression. That's also why so many of us run from God out of fear we can never live up to His high expectations.

> "But he said to me, 'My grace is sufficient for you, for my power is made perfect in weakness.' Therefore I will boast all the more gladly of my weaknesses, so that the power of Christ may rest upon me. For the sake of Christ, then, I am content with weaknesses, insults, hardships, persecutions, and calamities. For when I am weak, then I am strong" (2 Corinthians 12:9–10 NIV).

It's in our imperfections that we can most feel God's perfect love. It's in our weaknesses that we can most experience God's strength. It's in our confusion that we can most see God's wisdom.

Therefore, do not strive to be perfect. Simply strive to be in union with the only One who is.

DAY 19

MORE THAN ENOUGH

We all have something we desperately want in life—a relationship, a dream, a raise, a better body, etc.

We want this thing so badly, we believe we won't fully be happy until we get it. But the more we seem to chase after it, the further it seems to run from us. The more tightly we clutch something, the more easily it slips through our fingers.

> "If you cling to your life, you will lose it; but if you give it up for me, you will find it" (Matthew 10:39 NLT).

One of the most excruciating and liberating life lessons you'll ever experience is that God is enough.

A couple years ago, I went through an extremely painful breakup, feeling like I could not breathe without this person. Over time, I learned to grow close to God, help others, and find joy despite my pain. Once I got to that point where I didn't rely on the relationship anymore, the relationship was restored.

God often works this way to purify our hearts and test our faith. He'll wait until you don't *need* a relationship, to bring the perfect person into your life. He will wait until you don't *need* to be on Broadway, to give you the leading role. He will wait until you don't *need* that fancy apartment, to bless you with a raise at work.

"But seek first his kingdom and his righteousness,
and all these things will be given to you as well"
(Matthew 6:33).

"Take delight in the Lord, and he will give you
the desires of your heart" (Psalm 37:4 ESV).

Performers, remember this at your auditions. Don't be so focused on booking a job that you block the flow of God's energy through you. When you are content in God, you rely on His power, not yours. *That's* what people notice and will get you the job in the first place.

"I have learned the secret of being content in any
and every situation, whether well fed or hungry,
whether living in plenty or in want" (Philippians
4:13 NIV).

So what's the thing in your life you think you *need* right now to be happy? When you find your joy in God and realize He alone is enough, He will give you more than enough in return.

DAY 20

THE DIFFERENCE BETWEEN RIGHT AND RIGHT

We have this entitled mentality as a society, especially living in a country founded upon justice and rights. Though rights that uphold human dignity are good, rights that encourage human pride are bad.

We have every to right to yell at a lady who cuts in front of us at the store. We have every *right* to date and make out with as many people as we want while we're single. We have every *right* to hold a grudge and retaliate against someone who's hurt us. We have every *right* to gossip about a friend who mistreats us. We have every *right* to cheat a big corporation who cheats so many others. We have every *right* to sit at home and watch Netflix all day instead of helping a friend.

But God does not call us to exercise our rights. He calls us to exercise love, grace, mercy, forgiveness, patience, self-control, kindness, and generosity. Thus, just because you have the *right* to do something doesn't mean it's the *right* thing to do.

"I have the right to do anything, you say—but not everything is beneficial. I have the right to do anything—but not everything is constructive" (1 Corinthians 10:23 NIV).

"There is a way that appears to be right, but in the end it leads to death" (Proverbs 14:12 NIV).

Imagine if God acted upon everything He was entitled to. None of us would be here. Though we continuously turn our backs on God, He gave up his right to turn His back on us by sending His only son to love us, live among us, and die for us.

The apostle Paul also recognized the need to give up his rights for the sake of the Gospel:

"Since we have planted spiritual seed among you, aren't we entitled to a harvest of physical food and drink? If you support others who preach to you, shouldn't we have an even greater right to be supported? But we have never used this right. We would rather put up with anything than be an obstacle to the Good News about Christ" (Corinthians 9:11 ESV).

So the next time you get advice that starts with "you have every right to . . ." take pause and consider not what is most fair, but what is most beneficial.

DAY 21

COMFORT WITH SILENCE

I've always looked up to my mom. Socializing is her gift, and I grew up observing how masterfully she interacted with everyone from the store clerk to the CEO. Thus, I always gauged my own social aptitude by how well I could keep a conversation going and fill the silence. I always saw a lack of words as a weakness or a sign of incompatibility.

I approach my relationship with God in a similar way. A large part of my prayer time is spent with me do the talking. (Let's just say, I am not very good at the whole emptying my mind, meditation thing.) Then I expect God, like any good conversationalist, to keep the conversation going by answering me back right away. However, God's style of communicating is a bit different:

> "And after the earthquake there was a fire, but the LORD was not in the fire. And after the fire there was the sound of a gentle whisper" (1 Kings 19:12 NLT).

> "Be not rash with your mouth, nor let your heart be hasty to utter a word before God, for God is in

heaven and you are on earth. Therefore let your words be few" (Ecclesiastes 5:2 ESV).

"Better to hear the quiet words for a wise person than the shouts of a foolish king" (Ecclesiastes 9:17 NLT).

"When there are many words, transgression is unavoidable, but he who restrains his lips is wise" (Proverbs 10:19 NASB).

"Whoever restrains his words has knowledge, and he who has a cool spirit is a man of understanding. Even fools are thought wise if they keep silent, and discerning if they hold their tongues" (Proverbs 17:27–28 ESV).

"The Lord will fight for you, and you have only to be silent" (Exodus 14:14 ESV).

"Oh that you would be completely silent, and that it would become your wisdom" (Job 13:5 NASB)!

As I've gotten older, I've come to discover a real power in silence. For silence, itself, communicates far more than words. It communicates contentment, generosity, freedom, security, wisdom, and love.

The need to fill the silence can come from a desire to control a conversation, whether it's with another person or with God. Taking a pause to sit and reflect doesn't kill a conversation, it allows it to refresh itself, giving the other person an opportunity to take it in another direction. It also shows a person you are content to simply be in their presence without requiring anything more from the exchange.

I used to be sad when I saw older couples at a restaurant, not saying a word to each other. But perhaps, this is more a result of growing together than apart:

"We sit silently and watch the world around us. This has taken a lifetime to learn. It seems only the old are able to sit next to one another and not say anything and still feel content. The young, brash and impatient, must always break the silence. It is a waste, for silence is pure. Silence is holy. It draws people together because only those who are comfortable with each other can sit without speaking. This is the great paradox" (Nicholas Sparks).

I challenge you (and myself) to welcome silence in both our social and prayer lives, giving God space and room to move, refresh, and redirect our paths.

DAY 22

PLAY A SUPPORTING ROLE

Most of the time, we focus on our role as the leading character in our lives. We ask God to send people to support us, encourage us, and give us guidance along the way. While this is certainly valid, we rarely pause to think about the supporting role we play in other people's lives.

Think of all the people in your life that have enabled you to get to where you are today. In a vacuum, you never would have had the means, encouragement, or guidance they gave you. The same is true for all those you come across. God has put people, opportunities, knowledge, and resources in your path—not just for your sake—but for theirs.

> "Let each of you look not only to his own interests, but also to the interests of others" (Philippians 2:4).

> "In humility count others more significant than yourselves" (Philippians 2:3 ESV).

"Do not withhold good from those to whom it is due, when it is in your power to do it" (Proverbs 3:27 NIV).

"Let no one seek his own good, but the good of his neighbor" (1 Corinthians 10:24 ESV).

If you think about it, the power we have to contribute to another person's story is so exciting. Many times we think something good about a person, but never say it, not realizing what a profound impact a simple act can have.

It's incredible how the smallest word of encouragement, connecting someone to the right person, or simply lending a listening ear can change someone's entire narrative:

Do you see someone struggling in class or an audition? Give them a compliment . . . you may be the reason they don't give up on their dreams.

Do you know someone looking for a job? Putting them in touch with the right people could give them to means to stay in New York.

Do you know someone who is in a bad relationship, but everyone else is afraid to say something? Your loving guidance could save them from years of abuse or a bad marriage.

A supporting role can be the most rewarding role we ever play. And in making other's lives more beautiful, we're enhancing our own. The most legendary example of this? Jesus.

DAY 23

CRAVE

Sometimes our cravings are a sign that something else is missing.

For example, craving certain foods can indicate an underlying nutritional deficiency. Craving carbs can mean you're blood sugar's low, which can be remedied by eating more fiber. Craving sugar can mean you're dehydrated, which can be remedied by eating more water-based fruits. Craving salt can indicate high stress levels, which can be remedied by eating foods high in Vitamin B.

This same idea applies to all areas of our lives. The urge to return to a destructive relationship may indicate loneliness, a misplaced need for validation, or spiritual deficiency. The urge to get drunk or binge may come from feelings of failure, depression, or anxiety that we are trying to numb.

The good news is there's a type of multivitamin to help with all of these urges—God. Every morning, spend some time with God in His word and in prayer to make sure you have the nourishment you need to make it through the day. The root of many of our problems—confusion, struggles, worry, and despair—come from being malnourished spiritually.

"And my God will fully supply your every need according to his glorious riches in the Messiah Jesus" (Philippians 4:19–20 ISV).

"And God is able to give you more than you need, so that you will always have all you need for yourselves and more than enough for every good cause" (2 Corinthians 9:8 GNT).

"You, Lord, are all I have, and You give me all I need; my future is in Your hands. How wonderful are Your gifts to me; how good they are! I praise the Lord because He guides me, and in the night my conscience warns me. I am always aware of the Lord's presence; He is near, and nothing can shake me. And so I am thankful and glad, and I feel completely secure because You protect me from the power of death. I have served You faithfully, and You will not abandon me to the world of the dead. You will show me the path that leads to life; Your presence fills me with joy and brings me pleasure forever" (Psalm 16:5–11 GNT).

The more we experience God's abundant love and intimacy, the more we begin to crave Him alone. And as we do so, all our other longings are satisfied as well.

DAY 24

ALL USED UP

There are times in my life when I feel like a complete failure. No matter how good my intentions are, I end up letting myself, others, and God down.

In these moments, I feel like staying in bed with the lights off and just sleeping the days away. Instead of feeling usable by God, I feel all used up.

How can I give good advice if I can't even figure out my own life? How can I give others encouragement when I'm in the pit of despair? How can I write a post full of wisdom when I feel so clueless myself?

Today was one of those days. I felt broken, ashamed, disappointed in myself, and completely disqualified from being able to handle all God's entrusted me with. I realize it's only when I feel squeaky clean, blemish free, and holy that I believe God will bless me and others through me. Anytime I screw up, I feel unworthy of God's favor.

Not only is this mindset incorrect, it's unbiblical. In fact, God specializes in using "unusable" sinners. David committed adultery and murder, and God later said he was a man after his own heart.

Paul persecuted Christians, and went on to write half of the New Testament. Among countless others.

I saw this in action tonight. A dear friend of mine asked if I could pray with her about some things she's struggling with. Though that feeling of inadequacy swept over me, I readily agreed. We had a very lovely and intimate conversation, and God used both of us to speak truth into the other person's life. My feelings of inadequacy did not disqualify me from being used, they humbled me enough so God *could* use me. Same with her. While she may have thought I was doing her a favor, she really did me the favor. And we both experienced God's favor.

> "But for that very reason I was shown mercy so that in me, the worst of sinners, Christ Jesus might display his immense patience as an example for those who would believe in him and receive eternal life" (1 Timothy 1:16 NIV).

> "For just as through the disobedience of the one man the many were made sinners, so also through the obedience of the one man the many will be made righteous" (Romans 5:19).

> "Brothers, think of what you were when you were called. Not many of you were wise by human standards; not many were influential; not many were of noble birth" (1 Corinthians 1:26 NIV).

> "But God chose the foolish things of the world to shame the wise; God chose the weak things of the world to shame the strong. He chose the lowly things of this world and the despised things—and the things that are not—to nullify the things that are, so that no one may boast before him" (1 Corinthians 1:27–29 NIV).

If you're going through a dark time right now and don't feel particularly holy, pure, lovable, or close to God, realize that those are the opportunities for us to be closer to God than ever before.

So if you're feeling all used up, get ready. God's about to use you in a very powerful way.

DAY 25

CHUTES AND LADDERS

One of my favorite board games of all times is *Chutes and Ladders*. Yet, despite its fun simplicity, it can be extremely frustrating! Sometimes you get lucky and land on a huge ladder that lets to climb high above everyone else. And other times, you land on a huge slide that takes you all the way back to the bottom. Extreme highs and lows.

Life is a lot like that.

Sometimes you're moving along just fine and then something devastating happens. You lose a job, a relationship, a loved one, or a dream, and you slide down into despair. You feel like no matter how much time passes, you will forever be a lesser, more broken, and jaded version of yourself.

But what you don't see are the ladders of opportunity God has placed before you if you'll just continue to play. He knows that you have to be at the bottom of the ladder in order to climb to the top.

> "We are pressed on every side by troubles, but we are not crushed. We are perplexed, but not driven to despair. We are hunted down, but never abandoned by God. We get knocked down, but

we are not destroyed" (2 Corinthians 4:8–9 NLT).

There have been times in my life where I experienced so much emotional pain, I never thought I would recover. I thought I had ruined the fairytale life I'd imagined, and I wished I could just die and start over. But from that pain, God has given me immeasurably more joy in return.

"Yet what we suffer now is nothing compared to the glory he will reveal to us later" (Romans 8:18 NLT).

"So be truly glad. There is wonderful joy ahead, even though you must endure many trials for a little while" (1 Peter 1:6 NLT).

The pain did change me forever, but in such an incredible way. The struggles I thought were making me less of myself were actually giving me access to a greater dimension of myself I didn't know existed.

"Beloved, do not be surprised at the fiery trial when it comes upon you to test you, as though something strange were happening to you. But rejoice insofar as you share Christ's sufferings, that you may also rejoice and be glad when his glory is revealed" (1 Peter 4:12–19 ESV).

In fact, there have even been times when I felt like God was being way too generous. He doesn't hold back his blessings once we've healed. He keeps on going! He overflows us so we can pour out those blessings onto others.

"And we know that for those who love God all things work together for good, for those who are called according to his purpose" (Romans 8:28 NIV).

Instead of seeing pain as something to fear, embrace it as part of God's chiseling away process, getting you one step closer to the person you're meant to be.

So as you slide down the ladder, don't put your head in your hands, put your hands in the air! Cry deeply, choose love, and get ready to experience joy, countless revelations, and a life far beyond the one you imagined.

DAY 26

THE HALLWAY

It's easy to praise God during a relationship or a job opportunity, but what about in between? Perhaps, youre relationship just ended, and your now back to the dating game. Or perhaps, your show contract just ended, and you're back to the audition hustle. What do you do now?

Most of us choose one of two options—we either dwell on the glory days of the past, or we long for a future we've imagined. We miss out on the third and best option, to be fully present in the moment and to praise God in the hallway until he opens another door.

> "I will bless the Lord at all times: His praise shall continually be in my mouth. My soul shall make her boast in the Lord: the humble shall hear thereof, and be glad. O magnify the Lord with me, and let us exalt His name together. I sought the Lord, and He heard me, and delivered me from all my fears" (Psalm 34:1–5 KJV).

Open doors, opportunities, and relationships are blessings, no doubt. But it's in those neutral, in between, seemingly insignificant places that the real growth, character development, trust, exhilaration, faith, beauty, freedom, self-love, learning, and living occur. And unless we begin to embrace every single stage of life as crucial to our destinies, we won't be ready for what lies ahead.

> "Rejoice evermore. Pray without ceasing. In everything give thanks: for this is the will of God in Christ Jesus concerning you" (1 Thessalonians 5:16–18 KJV).

Our circumstances don't just bring about our thoughts. Our thoughts also bring about our circumstances. If we simply strive to remain both present and grateful—whether married, single, working, unemployed, healthy, sick, hungry, or full—we will bring about more of what we want and squeeze out every ounce of life along the way.

For those of you who have just lost a relationship or a job and are feeling down and crushed, put all your focus into falling in love with yourself and everything around you. Sadness, bitterness, and reminiscing will only keep you knocking down the closed door instead of moving toward the open one.

We're really good at investing in others but often forget to invest in the two relationships that are constant—our relationship with God and with ourselves.

So it's time to throw a party in the hallway! Put on some exhilarating music. *Laugh a lot!* Sit outside with your eyes closed, breathe in the air, and smile. Experience the romance of being fully alive—a state of being far above any trial or triumph.

Fall madly in love with God. Fall madly in love with yourself. Other people and things will come and go. As long as you're having a blast along the way, the next one will be right around the corner, asking you for the next dance.

DAY 27

THE ART OF UNLEARNING

If you only learn one thing from this message, it's unlearn.

When trying to become who we really are we usually think of what we need to add to ourselves—skills, schools, degrees, jobs, people, and anything else that will help shape our identities.

But somewhere on the path to finding ourselves we lose ourselves. The pressures and practicalities of life force us to add so many worldly layers, our truest selves get buried underneath it all.

In addition to learning the things necessary to develop our skills, we also learn bad habits, toxic relationships, societal norms, cultural customs, addictions, a desire to control, and how to fear. We end up robotic and numb or lost and ashamed, wondering where our childhood dreams went wrong.

The truth is God knew you before you were born. You already arrived in this world with an identity and everything you needed inside you. He created you with a purpose, and for a purpose, which no employer or casting director can disqualify you from fulfilling.

> "Before I formed you in the womb I knew you,
> before you were born I set you apart; I appointed

you as a prophet to the nations" (Jeremiah 1:5 ESV).

So becoming who you truly are has little to do with learning more, but rather unlearning everything that is not true within you. Those other things you picked up along the way are *not* a part of your identity. They are simply hiding your identity from you.

> "For God hath not given us the spirit of fear, but of power and of love and of a sound mind" (2 Timothy 1:7 KJV).

Think back to when you were a child. What did you love? What was your personality? What were your dreams? How often did you play? How often did you laugh? In other words, reflect on who you were before the world diluted you down.

> "What you seek is already within you. You uncover it by shedding all that is untrue within you" (Sampo Kasila).

So stop trying so hard to create your identity, and instead shed the things that conceal your identity. Unlearn the impulse to fear, the need to control, the limits of practicality, the pressure to grow up and settle for that job, the idea that your dreams are foolish.

Then as you strip all of that extra stuff away, you just might find you inside.

DAY 28

GOOD NEWS BEARERS

Sometimes we think the only way to be a good witness to God is by sharing the positive things happening in our lives. We praise Him for the new job, the new relationship, the new apartment.

While this is very right and good, we often miss opportunities to demonstrate the unshakable joy of faith in our struggles—praising Him despite a job loss, relationship ending, or hard living situation. In truth, your outlook during the hard times is often a greater witness to the power of God in your life than in the good times.

The past week, I've been moping around all morose, blaming a broken heart and a bout of bronchitis. While it's OK to be down from time to time, I realized I was missing a powerful opportunity to demonstrate the benefit of my faith in the midst of my pain. I could either choose to be overcome by it or overcome it. I could suffer under the weight of the full burden or give some of it over to Jesus.

The beauty of faith is it gives you this choice. Faith doesn't mean you stop feeling sadness, guilt, fear, envy, or loneliness; it means you won't be overwhelmed by them. Faith doesn't mean you become less broken, but that you become more aware of your brokenness and need for a Savior. God doesn't promise us that life will be easy for those who believe. But He does promise to help us through whatever comes.

> "Consider it pure joy, my brothers and sisters, whenever you face trials of many kinds, because you know that the testing of your faith produces perseverance" (James 1:2–3 NIV).

> "I have told you these things, so that in me you may have peace. In this world you will have trouble. But take heart! I have overcome the world" (John 16:33 NIV).

> "May the God of hope fill you with all joy and peace in believing, so that by the power of the Holy Spirit you may abound in hope" (Romans 15:13 ESV).

In the book, *The Ragamuffin Gospel*, the author points out that true faith also means fully accepting God's free gift of mercy and forgiveness—that walking around with an overly gloomy, self-condemning, and defeatist attitude contradicts the good news of salvation we claim to believe:

> "Yes, we feel guilt over sins, but healthy guilt is one which acknowledges the wrong done and feels remorse, but then is free to embrace the forgiveness that has been offered. Healthy guilt focuses on the realization that all has been forgiven, the wrong has been redeemed" (Brennan Manning).

In a world that bears so much bad news, we need to bear the Good News of faith by how we respond. May our lives unconditionally reflect God's unconditional love.

> "Proclaim the good news of His salvation from day to day" (Psalm 96:2 NKJV).

DAY 29

PUT DOWN YOUR PENCILS

We desperately want to write our own life stories. We have very specific ideas in our heads of what belongs and what doesn't—from subplots, characters, and settings to what this person will say, how we will achieve that dream, and how many chapters we get for each stage in our lives.

When our story does not play out as we've written it, we become disappointed, discouraged, and even depressed. We begin to feel like because things do not go according to plan, the story's over.

However, the disappointments in our lives are not a plot problem, character problem, or time problem. They're an author problem.

> "For my thoughts are not your thoughts, neither are your ways my ways, declares the Lord. For as the heavens are higher than the earth, so are my ways higher than your ways and my thoughts than your thoughts" (Isaiah 55:8–9 NIV).

"Many are the plans in the mind of a man, but it is the purpose of the Lord that will stand" (Proverbs 16:9 ESV).

For example, have you ever caught yourself imagining how a specific scene in your life should play out?

You see a cute person on the subway, and you begin to think how perfect would it be if they sat down next to you, struck up a conversation, and that's how you'll tell your kids you met. (Then they nonchalantly walk past you and get off at the next stop.)

Or you have an awesome callback and later see a call from a mysterious number. You imagine it being the casting director offering you the job and this being the role that launches your Broadway career. (Instead, it's only a telemarketer, and you never hear about the job.)

Whenever I find myself suggesting my own ideas to God, I imagine Him smiling and lovingly responding: You think *that's* a good story? *I'll show you a good story!*

"Now to Him who is able to do far more abundantly than all that we ask or think, according to the power at work within us" (Ephesians 3:20 ESV).

Don't try to write your story. Don't compare your story to others. Don't desire the stories in movies. The story God's writing for you will be better than any bestselling novel or box office hit. It will be full of more romance, comedy, action, suspense, adventure, twists and turns, than you ever thought possible in one lifetime.

The best part? You get to play the lead. If only you are willing to be led.

DAY 30

THOU SHALT

People can tell who we are by our actions.

How do you know someone's a dancer? They dance.

How do you know someone's an actor? They act.

How do you know someone's a teacher? They teach.

How do you know someone's a Christian? . . .

We have a long set of rules about what being a Christian is *not*. As long as we do not do this, do not go there, do not say that, we figure that's all it takes.

Likewise, people in the Old Testament became accustomed to the "Thou shalt not" version of God. Thou shalt not steal, commit adultery, worship idols, kill, or swear.

When Jesus came, He put a lot of emphasis on "Thou shalt"—thou shalt love thy God, thou shalt love thy neighbor, thou shalt forgive 70 × 7 times, thou shalt care for the poor.

How do know someone's a football player? . . . Because they refuse to play tennis? No, it's because they choose to play football.

Admittedly, choosing not to do something we feel is wrong is absolutely necessary in living out our faith. In this society, and especially in this business, you will have to opt out of many things that violate your conscience. But we must not reduce our faith to the absence of negative action, rather than the presence of positive action.

> "But someone will say, 'You have faith and I have works.' Show me your faith apart from your works, and I will show you my faith by my works" (James 2:18 NKJV).

Jesus was far more known for what he *did* do than what he *did not* do. He was known for eating with tax collectors, not for refusing to associate with them. He was known for healing on the Sabbath day, not refusing to defile it. He was known for turning water into wine, not refusing to drink.

> "In the same way, let your light shine before others, so that they may see your good works and give glory to your Father who is in heaven" (Matthew 5:16 ESV).

Following in his example, people should tell we're Christians by our actions. Not because we don't swear, but because we give up our weekend to help a friend move apartments. Not because we refuse to go to the bars, but because we go and have uplifting, meaningful conversations. Not because we refuse to play a role, but because we respectfully question certain choices made and then transform the role.

> "What good is it, my brothers, if someone says he has faith but does not have works? Can that faith save him? If a brother or sister is poorly clothed and lacking in daily food, and one of you says to them, "Go in peace, be warmed and filled," without giving them the things needed for the body, what good is that? So also faith by itself, if it does not have works, is dead" (James 2:14–17 ESV).

Let's not hide behind a faith that's passive, stagnant, legalistic, and fearful, but one that's active, in motion, from the heart, and bold. The purpose our faith is not to show others that we love God but to show others that God loves them!

So how do you know someone's a Christian? They don't just know Christ. They make Christ known.

DAY 31

CALLING ALL REBELS!

What makes artists awesome is we all have a rebel inside us. We want to create new things, be original, stand out, say something. We like to think we're different, more progressive, more liberal than the stiff suits on Wall Street.

Why then are we constantly falling prey to an industry full of worldly clichés and moral compromises?

Friends, to be honest, this industry controls us like puppets on a string. It has utterly convinced us that to achieve success, we need to wear this, talk like that, please him, impress her, sign with this person, work with that person, take this class, hire this teacher, go to this audition, and on and on and on and on and on and on and on . . .

And you know what? In order to achieve their definition of success, they're right. But if you define success not by *what* you do, but *how* you do it and *who* you are, then they are sorely mistaken.

> "For what does it profit a man to gain the whole
> world and forfeit his soul" (Mark 8:36 ESV)?

Throughout all history—and especially in our world today—*love* is the most radical and underutilized form of rebellion. Jesus, the ultimate lover, was the ultimate rebel. He very *easily* could have buttered up the religious leaders and political figures and watered down his convictions to get ahead. Instead, he hung out with sinners, redeemed prostitutes, and lived on the street. He proved that rebellion is even more powerful through love than through hate.

> "Don't copy the behavior and customs of this world, but let God transform you into a new person by changing the way you think. Then you will learn to know God's will for you, which is good and pleasing and perfect" (Romans 12:2 NLT).

When we were teenagers, it was cool to see someone with ripped jeans, smoking a cigarette, rapping hateful messages, having sex, giving the finger, not caring about anyone or anything. But now, when I see these things over and over again in our industry, I don't see a rebel. I see a cliché. I see a mascot. Hate, sex, and drugs are *not* sexy, guys. They're just hate, sex, and drugs.

But when I see someone turn down a role because it violates their integrity, or when I see someone choreographing a masterful, moving piece of work without relying on a single gyration, or I see someone putting their family before taking on an extra job that will further their career . . . *then* I see a true rebel. I see a revolutionary. I see a leader. I see an artist. Love, selflessness, and integrity are the sexiest, most attractive things in the entire world.

At the Teen's Choice awards, Ashton Kutcher—admitting his name was really "Chris" Kutcher—gave one of the most moving, brutally honest, and refreshing acceptance speeches I've ever heard:

"The sexiest thing in the entire world is being really smart, and being thoughtful, and being generous. Everything else is crap. I promise you! It's just crap that people try to sell to you to make you feel like less. So don't buy it! Be smart. Be thoughtful. Be generous."

"When you grow up, you tend to be told that world is the way that it is and that your job is to live your life inside the world . . . but life can be a lot broader than that when you realize one simple thing: you can build your own things, and you can build your own life that other people can live in. So don't just live a life. Build one."

Fellow artists, refuse to become a tool in the devil's hands. We need to reclaim who we are, even at the expense or delay of achievement. Because I promise you, with the almighty God on your side, you can achieve infinitely more than you can without Him.

> "Now all glory to God who is able to do immeasurably more than all we ask or imagine, according to His power that is at work within us" (Ephesians 3:20 ESV).

DAY 32

FULL TANK

We always hear, "love your neighbor as yourself," but it should also work the other way around— love yourself as your neighbor.

> "Whoever gets sense loves his own soul; he who keeps understanding will discover good" (Proverbs 19:8 ESV).

> "For no one ever hated his own flesh, but nourishes and cherishes it, just as Christ does the church" (Ephesians 5:29 NKJV).

A good friend of mine made a very wise comment tonight. She said we know how to love ourselves better than anyone else. We know what makes us tick, what inspires us, what brings us joy, and what makes us feel alive.

So often we rely on another person to give us the love we need. But no person, however wonderful, will be able to read our minds, do everything right, know exactly what makes us happy, or love us perfectly. Only God can do that.

Relationships fall apart, not because people are incompatible, but because we're putting way too much pressure on one imperfect person to meet the needs of a totally different imperfect person.

But when we have our own love supply, through God's Word and kind words to ourselves, any love on top of that is simply bonus. And once we learn to love ourselves, something wonderful happens . . .

We not only have more love to freely give, we are able to freely accept or let go of love from others. We are no longer imprisoned by fear, guilt, hate, bitterness, resentment because someone didn't show us love. We already have a full tank.

We become stable, complete, consistent, and secure—regardless of who decides to walk in and out of our lives.

> "And God will generously provide all you need. Then you will always have everything you need and plenty left over to share with others" (2 Corinthians 9:8 NLT).

Loving yourself is not selfish. It's your responsibility. It helps perfect your love for others. You cannot give what you don't have. So love yourself spiritually with scripture and prayer. Love yourself physically with food from the earth and activity. Love yourself emotionally with hearty laughs and deep cries.

Have you recently experienced a breakup, a job loss, or any other conflict? Never withhold love from yourself or others, no matter the circumstance.

For the more freely you love, the more freely you live.

> "Let all that you do be done in love" (1 Corinthians 16:14 ESV).

DAY 33

VEGETABLES FIRST

There's a reason your mom told you to finish your vegetables before getting dessert. She wasn't being mean; she was simply more concerned with you getting what you needed rather than getting what you wanted. She knew that if you filled up on the things you wanted, you wouldn't have any room left over in your stomach for the things you needed.

This is also how God operates with us. He wants us to be able to enjoy dessert, but not at the expense of first receiving true nourishment. He knows if he gave us everything we ask for before letting us develop the virtues we need, our characters would suffer. We wouldn't have room for patience, faith, mercy, generosity, hope, and love.

> "The Lord will guide you always; he will satisfy your needs in a sun-scorched land and will strengthen your frame. You will be like a well-watered garden, like a spring whose waters never fail" (Isaiah 58:11 NIV).

Studies suggest that the reason for obesity in our country is not just that we're overeating, but that we're starving. Though we're eating mass quantities of food, we eat very little of the things our bodies actually need to feel good and function optimally.

All day, my body has been craving a big bowl of steamed vegetables. But rather than take time to prepare them, I've been munching on other, less nutritious things. After a while, I became too filled up with other stuff to make room for the one thing my body really needed.

This also happens in our relationship with God. Our spirits are starving for a life-giving union with the Father; for tranquility and peace in our fast-paced lives. Yet instead of starting each day with prayer and Scripture, we feast on Facebook for breakfast, demands at work for lunch, and TV shows for dinner. So by the end of the day, we are filled to the max with little room left for things that benefit us most.

> "Nevertheless, I will bring health and healing to it; I will heal my people and will let them enjoy abundant peace and security" (Jeremiah 33:6 NIV).

It's proven that the first hour you're awake will determine the rest of your day. So I encourage you to try an experiment:

For one week, spend the first moments you're awake reading the Bible or a devotion and eating a veggie-packed breakfast. You'll go into your day with all the spiritual and physical nourishment you need, so anything else you want is an enhancement, not a substitute.

You may even find that when you're getting what you need, you crave less of what you do not.

> "Test your servants for ten days; let us be given vegetables to eat and water to drink [. . .] At the end of ten days it was seen that they were better in appearance and fatter in flesh than all the youths who ate the king's food. So the steward took away their food and the wine they were to drink, and gave them vegetables" (Daniel 1:12–16 NIV).

DAY 34

SOUL MAINTENANCE

Today I got a massage that a friend bought for me two years ago. Due to my limited experience and a couple underwhelming massages in the past, I did not have high expectations. Usually, I find them too soft and weak, so I end up leaving more tense, knowing I just paid for something less than necessary.

But this massage was truly glorious, including sixty minutes of deep tissue, full-body, and hot stones (Taiji Body Work). It had the perfect amount of firmness and intensity, leaving me feeling completely renewed, reinvigorated, and restored.

I couldn't help but compare this experience with God's love for us. His perfect love is firm, yet loving. It both serves and transforms. It helps us work through all the sore spots and places of tension in our lives. Though uncomfortable at times, it always leaves us better than when we began.

"For whom the LORD loves He reproves, even
as a father corrects the son in whom he delights"
(Proverbs 3:12 NASB).

Without us having to say a word, God can tell which areas of our life have the most knots and require the most attention—even if we're not aware of them ourselves. He will diligently rub them out until we learn to relax and let go of their hold on us.

During the massage, some moments were less comfortable than others. But I found that especially in the more tense places, the key is to relax and breathe in order to minimize the pain. The more we surrender to God the tough places, the more peace we have and the more effectively He can work.

> "For momentary, light affliction is producing for us an eternal weight of glory far beyond all comparison" (2 Corinthians 4:17–18 NASB).

I also noticed that the smaller muscles and tendons were more sensitive than the larger ones. When the masseuse rubbed out my Achilles tendons and neck, they were much more tender and sensitive than when she did my hamstrings or shoulder blades.

Similarly, while most of us don't struggle with larger sins like murder, we struggle to let go of the smaller, destructive habits like overeating. These are often much harder to let go of and let God change.

> "Search me, O God, and know my heart! Try me and know my thoughts! And see if there be any grievous way in me, and lead me in the way everlasting" (Psalm 139:23–24 ESV)!

After the massage, I realized the only cash I had on me was $7 for the tip. I figured I could make up for it by verbalizing how much I enjoyed her services. Though the masseuse graciously accepted, the look of disappointment on her face was apparent.

The manager behind the desk said they ask for a $10 tip for their employees but not to worry about it this time. However, the massage brought me so much healing and joy, it was a no brainer to go get cash at a nearby ATM and go back to give her an extra $5.

God gives to us freely and doesn't legally require anything specific in return, but I wonder if the same look of disappointment comes across his face when we don't take time to show our appreciation.

How do we do this? By loving others. Speaking our gratitude to God is great. Showing our gratitude is even better.

> "Therefore, since we receive a kingdom which cannot be shaken, let us show gratitude, by which we may offer to God an acceptable service with reverence and awe; for our God is a consuming fire" (Hebrews 12:28–29 NASB).

> "Dear children, let us not love with words or speech but with actions and in truth" (1 John 3:16–18 NASB).

Some may consider a physical massage a luxury, but when it comes to matters of the soul, I believe we should daily stretch out on the altar of grace and ask God to lovingly soften the hard spots.

> May God's love pamper, heal, and transform you—so that you may "go and do likewise" (Luke 10:37 NIV).

DAY 35

MY WAY OR THE HIGH WAY

I always assume my will is the opposite of God's will. If I want something so badly, I automatically suspect God will require me to give it up as a test of my love and obedience to Him. Sometimes I'm even hesitant to pray for Him to reveal His will because I'm afraid of what it might require of me.

This self-sacrificial and fearful mindset is not only a misunderstanding of Scripture, but of God himself.

> "Delight yourself in the Lord, and He will give you the desires of your heart" (Psalm 37:4 ESV).

> "For I know the plans I have for you declares the Lord. Plans to prosper you and not to harm you. Plans to give you a hope and a future" (Jeremiah 29:11 NIV).

> "May He give you the desire of your heart and make all your plans succeed" (Psalm 20:4).

A few weeks back, I listened to a sermon on discovering God's will for your life. The pastor said rather than focusing on the part of God's will you don't know, focus on the part He's already revealed to you: the guidelines in the Bible, God's Commandments, Jesus's teachings, and most importantly, to love God and others with all our hearts.

"It is God's will that you should be sanctified: that you should avoid sexual immorality" (1 Thessalonians 4:3 NIV).

"For it is God's will that by doing good you should silence the ignorant talk of foolish people" (1 Peter 2:15 NIV).

When we are faithful in what God has revealed, our hearts become more aligned with the father, and we become better able to discern what He has not yet revealed.

Thus, the last step in following God's will is: "Love and do what you want" (St. Augustine).

In my experience, I feel much more close to the Father and fruitful when I am doing what makes me come alive. As Fr. James Martin says, "The most powerful form of evangelization is a joyful person." If your life does not bring you joy, it cannot bring joy to others.

"The glory of God is man fully alive" (Saint Irenaeus).

Likewise, Pastor Erwin McManus says, "God is not here to take life away from you but to give it more abundantly." Thus, we can only conclude that if God wants us to go down a certain path, He will give us the desire to do so.

One of my biggest fears is God calling me to be a nun. Ever since I was a little girl, I've deeply desired to have a husband and family, so I am terrified by the possibility that God might require me to give those up.

However, I believe that when we desire what is pleasing to God, He desires what is pleasing to us. It brings a Father great joy to bring joy to His children.

> "If you then, though you are evil, know how to give good gifts to your children, how much more will your Father in heaven give good gifts to those who ask him" (Matthew 7:11 NIV)!

So what's God's will? That we learn to love like Jesus. Perhaps, He is more concerned with our purpose than our profession.

Bottom line—God's will for us will never involve a lack of passion. Quite the opposite! We must have such passion for what we're going that we're willing to suffer for it in order to bear the most fruit.

DAY 36

A TIME TO LAUGH

Today, I went to confession. When I finished and was leaving the room, the priest cheerfully exclaimed, "So how excited are you for Easter?!" I let out a refreshing laugh and thanked him for his joy, to which he responded with another hearty chuckle.

Instead of leaving that room somberly, I walked out of there with a huge smile on my face, much to the surprise of the other penitents in line. My focus went from feeling badly for what I had done to feeling awesome about what Jesus had done.

Many of us think that the more spiritual we are, the more-mild mannered and profound we need to be. Some religious people feel the need to rise above humor, seeing it as something foolish and trivial. But I think it's the ones who are able to rise above their circumstances and find joy in everything who possess true intelligence and maturity. The closer we are to God, the more alive and joyful we become.

> "A sense of humor . . . is needed armor. Joy in one's heart and some laughter on one's lips is a sign that the person down deep has a pretty good grasp of life" (Hugh Sidey).

"A person without a sense of humor is like a wagon without springs. It's jolted by every pebble on the road" (Henry Ward Beecher).

We forget that God Himself is a playful Creator—just look around! Jesus had a tremendous sense of humor which drew people in. So many of the saints had a sense of humor, even while being martyred. Some of our most respected presidents were known for their wit and charisma.

"If I were two-faced, would I be wearing this one" (Abraham Lincoln)?

"From silly devotions and sour-faced saints, good Lord, deliver us" (St. Teresa of Avila).

The more seriously we take God, the less seriously we take ourselves and our problems. The more we exude God's joy, the more others are drawn to us and want what we have.

Humor unifies, disarms, and heals us. It releases endorphins in the body and delivers medicine to the soul. Humor gives us tremendous power because it puts grief, pain, and fear in their proper places. It reduces the shadow on the wall to the tiny little object that created it.

"She is clothed with strength and dignity, and she laughs without fear of the future" (Proverbs 31:25 NLT).

"A joyful heart is good medicine, but a crushed spirit dries up the bones" (Proverbs 17:22 ESV).

We so often associate humor, laughter, silliness, and playfulness with children. But have you ever noticed how the elderly tend to resurrect these qualities? I think it's because their perspective on life changes.

"Truly I tell you, unless you change and become like little children, you will never enter the kingdom of heaven" (Matthew 18:3 NIV).

Therefore, may we learn to laugh, play, and have fun as if our lives depended on it.

"So I recommend having fun, because there is nothing better for people in this world than to eat, drink, and enjoy life. That way they will experience some happiness along with all the hard work Go gives them under the sun" (Ecclesiastes 8:15 NLT).

DAY 37

THE CHALLENGE IS
IN THE CHASTE

We often want what we can't have. If someone treats us poorly, we work even harder to win their affection. We don't value those who treat us well but take them for granted, assuming they will always be there. This goes for guys and girls. Romantic relationships and friendships.

The more of a jerk a guy is and the more bratty a girl is, the more attractive they becomes to us. They become more mysterious, challenging, and desirable.

But let me ask you a question. All these qualities you find desirable before marriage, will they be desirable *after* marriage? Ladies, do you really want a guy that will ignore you, try his wit on other women, risk losing you, or walk out on your kids? Men, do you really want a woman whose confidence relies on her physical appearance and attention from others to be your life partner?

> "An excellent wife who can find? She is far more
> precious than jewels. The heart of her husband

trusts in her, and he will have no lack of gain. She does him good, and not harm, all the days of her life" (Proverbs 31:10–12 ESV).

We need to *stop* buying into cultural and media ideal of finding a mate. They are *wrong*. They are appealing to our animalistic instincts, when true love and marriage are built on the opposite—character, virtues, and commitment.

> "Love is patient, love is kind. It does not envy, it does not boast, it is not proud. It does not dishonor others, it is not self-seeking, it is not easily angered, it keeps no record of wrongs. Love does not delight in evil but rejoices with the truth. It always protects, always trusts, always hopes, always perseveres" (1 Corinthians 13:4–7 NLT).

Movies tell us the "spark" is rare. It's not. To be honest, you can have that spark with just about anyone. Shoot, you can feel a spark with a handsome, charismatic serial killer. Does that mean you should marry that person? *No!*

What's rare is someone who will stay by your side no matter what happens. Someone who loves you for exactly who you are without trying to change you according to their preferences. *That* is the type of person you should be friends with. *That* is the type of person you should marry.

Of course, a good marriage will also have passion—in fact, much, much more! If passion is a spark, commitment is a match. You want to marry someone with a lifetime supply, not someone who is easily snuffed out. You want to marry someone capable of relighting the flame, over and over again, when it inevitably flickers in the winds of life.

As my pastor says, "When you marry someone, they *become* the one." Don't be fooled into thinking that a spark with someone else who comes along means you missed out on true love. Remember, sparks are a dime a dozen. Commitment and faithfulness are the most precious, sexy, and romantic qualities you can find.

If you go to the gym and see a cute person with a great body, looking you up and down, and giving you butterflies, should you start fantasizing about your future? Well, depends on the future you want. However, if you're running down the street and drop all your things, and a guy stops to help you pick them up and then hails you a cab—that's a good place to start.

Also, don't fall for flattering words. Fake love may be blind, but true love is deaf. You know someone loves you not by their words, but by their actions.

> "His speech was smoother than butter, but his heart was war; His words were softer than oil, yet they were drawn swords" (Psalm 55:21 GWT).

Friends, we have to train ourselves to distinguish the alluring lie from the life-giving truth. We are subconsciously discarding the real treasure for the sake of the counterfeit. We are falling into lust and calling it love. No wonder divorce has almost become an unwritten wedding vow!

> "Do not conform to the pattern of this world, but be transformed by the renewing of your mind. Then you will be able to test and approve what God's will is—His good, pleasing, and perfect will" (Romans 12:2).

So, lovers, take it slow. It will save you a lot of extra pain, disappointment, and heartache. Chemistry is felt in an instant, and often, but character takes time to see fully.

The real challenge is not in the chase, it's in finding someone worth chasing. Take your time. Test every spark. You and your life's happiness are worth the wait.

DAY 38

BLESSED TO BLESS

There is not one single thing God has given you just for yourself. God doesn't bless those who have earned it; He blesses those who He can trust to bless others.

> "God has given each of you a gift from his great variety of spiritual gifts. Use them well to serve one another" (1 Peter 4:10 NLT).

In the arts, as in any business, it is easy to get caught up in how we can develop our gifts to get *ourselves* ahead. We're missing the point. And others are missing out!

Perhaps, God has given you a gift for music. Though He certainly delights in seeing you get pleasure from playing alone in your room, just imagine the children who would benefit from your instruction and be kept off the streets.

Perhaps, God has blessed you with being able to pick up choreography quickly. I'll bet you that isn't just so you can book a job, but also so that you can meet with someone outside of rehearsal to catch them up.

Perhaps, God has blessed you with the gift of humor. It's probably not just so you can make a lot of friends, but also so that you can *be* a friend and lift the spirits of someone going through a hard time.

I love how my pastor put it a few weeks ago. Suppose you give the UPS guy a package to deliver to your friend, but instead he keeps it at his house. He was never the intended recipient, and he did not complete his job.

Likewise, when we keep our gifts to ourselves, we don't complete the job God has given us. God has called us to be his hands and feet here on earth, each using what He has put in us to love to others. Don't underuse your gifts and deprive both yourself and others of their full potential.

Here's the most beautiful thing—when we use our gifts to bless others, we enjoy them more ourselves. Imagine a child gets a board game as a gift for Christmas. He will never enjoy the full benefits of the game until he agrees to share it with his brother.

> "Whoever brings blessing will be enriched,
> and one who waters will himself be watered"
> (Proverbs 11:25 ESV).

Artists, I will tell you a secret. Using your gifts to help others, even one person, even in secret, with a loving, generous spirit is the most *incredible high* you will ever experience in your entire artistic career. And guess what? It's an act you can perform every single day of your life.

May your faithfulness with the blessings you're given lead to countless more.

DAY 39

AIM HIGHER

We all have high aspirations in this industry, and we make it the sole purpose in our lives to achieve them. We spend all our time, money, and energy into achieving our dreams, believing we won't be happy until we've made them a reality.

While having goals and pursuing your passions are good, godly things, when we allow them to become the main focus in our lives, they go from being God-given to God-replacing. Rather than maintaining their proper place and giving us joy, they become idols that rob us of joy.

> "Do not lay up for yourselves treasures on earth, where moth and rust destroy and where thieves break in and steal, but lay up for yourselves treasures in Heaven, where neither moth nor rust destroys and where thieves do not break in and steal. For where your treasure is, there your heart will be also" (Matthew 6:19–21 NIV).

Let's say your dream is to become a famous singer. You think that once you attain this goal you will finally start to live. Based on the large number of celebrities that die young, abuse drugs, and suffer from depression, this is clearly not the case.

Friends, we only get one shot at this thing called life. Do you really want the pinnacle of your existence to be that Broadway musical you were in?

Now please don't get me wrong. God absolutely wants you to pursue the dreams He's put on your heart. It brings Him much pleasure when He can bless you with opportunities that bring you much pleasure!

But He doesn't want you to get so caught up in the worldly things that you miss out on the bigger purposes He's placed inside you. In other words, God is not asking you to settle for less than your dreams, He is asking you to *aim much higher!* He doesn't want to merely meet your expectations; He wants to *exceed* them!

> "Now glory be to God, by his mighty power at work within us is able to do far more than we would ever dare to ask or even dream of—infinitely beyond our highest prayers, desires, thoughts, or hopes" (Ephesians 3:20 NASB).

A dear friend of mine puts this principle into practice quite beautifully. Even after having a successful musical theater career in NYC, he didn't stop there. He established an international organization called Promethean Spark, which trains artists to teach life skills through dance. He continues to successfully pursue his musical theater dreams, but knows to make his greater calling a priority.

Maybe your greater calling is not to become the founder of a big nonprofit organization. Maybe it's not religious-based or glamorous. Perhaps your calling is to bring more of God's love into a city of people who are lonely, broken, and hurting. Or to raise godly children, mentor others, or master relationships.

In fact, the legacy we leave behind by leading an "obscure" life is often greater than that of leading a "famous" life.

Just think of the life of Jesus. He did not have a high-profile calling at the time. He hung out with everyday people, spent time with sinners, and made time to love people one-on-one, face-to-face. His low-profile life led to the greatest and most influential legacy known to man.

So please, continue to pursue your dreams so that the faithfulness of God may be magnified through you. Just realize they are merely a topping, not the cake.

> "I press on to reach the end of the race and receive
> the heavenly prize for which God, through Jesus
> Christ, is calling us" (Philippians 3:14 NLT).

When you begin to live like this, you become free of the pressure to succeed in this industry because you're already succeeding infinitely more in your higher calling every day.

And while you're busy living out God's dream for your life, it's amazing how your own dreams just fall into place.

> "I am the Lord, the God of all mankind. Is
> anything too hard for me" (Jeremiah 32:27
> NLT)?

DAY 40

THERMOSTAT LEADERS

Especially when it comes to presidential elections, we are quick to criticize political leaders. But we must ask ourselves, what kind of leaders are we in our circles of influence? Do strive to stand up or go along?

I love the analogy of choosing to be a thermometer Christian or thermostat Christian. Thermometers simply reflect the temperature of their surroundings, but thermostats change the temperature.

Artists, it's time to turn up the heat! We desperately need more people in positions of power who are not ruled by the world, but by the Lord. Those whose consciences are far louder than their egos. Who aren't so tightly enslaved by fear, greed, and pride, but are willing to risk losing worldly status for the sake of the greater good.

I recently watched a documentary about the prevalence of rape on college campuses. But even more shocking than the rapes themselves was the lack of action taken by school leaders. Most are so concerned with the reputation of the school, the fame of their athletes, or losing funds from alumni, they fail to protect the students they claim to care so much about.

"It is an abomination for kings to commit wicked acts, for a throne is established on righteousness" (Proverbs 16:12 NASB).

Like these school leaders, many of us try to save our reputations by covering up the truth, but we end up ruining our reputations in the process. As a parent, I would much rather send my child to a college where they acknowledged and buckled down on this issue, rather than one that parades a false sense of security.

"When the righteous increase, the people rejoice, but when a wicked man rules, people groan" (Proverbs 29:2 ESV).

Take Pontius Pilate, for example. He knew that Jesus was innocent. He knew it was wrong to put him to death. But since he did not fear God, his fear of the people and damaging his reputation won out. Again, in trying to preserve his name, he tarnished it for all of history. And he is still one of the most well-known antagonists in a story told over two thousand years later.

"Furthermore, you shall select out of all the people able men who fear God, men of truth, those who hate dishonest gain; and you shall place these over them as leaders of thousands, of hundreds, of fifties and of tens" (Exodus 18:21 NASB).

On the other hand, consider one of the most beloved leaders of our world today, Pope Francis. He's not interested in the various perks of the job, like living in the Vatican. He's not concerned with getting his hands dirty, but washes feet. He's not concerned with religious division, but welcomes all people with open arms. He also speaks the truth in love, which doesn't seek to offend but to affirm. His style of leadership is modeled after the best leader who ever lived—Jesus.

"It is not this way among you, but whoever wishes to become great among you shall be your servant" (Matthew 20:26 NASB).

Good, effective leadership does not command, it serves. It does not compete, it collaborates. It is not fear-driven, but love-driven. It doesn't not claim to know everything, but seeks the truth in everything. It does not only focus on *what* gets done, but *how* things get done. It does not shout, it listens. It does not strive to master others, but to master itself. It does not become a character, but has character.

God is not a Republican or Democrat. He is not conservative or liberal. He is simply a humanitarian and servant, desiring for all peoples and parties to behave and elect leaders accordingly.

"For an overseer, as God's steward, must be above reproach. He must not be arrogant or quick-tempered or a drunkard or violent or greedy for gain, but hospitable, a lover of good, self-controlled, upright, holy, and disciplined. He must hold firm to the trustworthy word as taught, so that he may be able to give instruction in sound doctrine and also to rebuke those who contradict it. For there are many you are insubordinate, empty talkers, and deceivers, especially those of the circumcision party. They must be silenced, since they are upsetting whole families by teaching for shameful gain what they ought not to teach" (Titus 1:7–14 ESV).

Decide to become a thermostat leader today, leading first by example. Your influence has nothing to do with status and everything to do with your heart.

May God lead us as we strive to lead others, giving us the discernment and courage to stand up for what is right, however unpopular or unprofitable it might be. May we choose what is wise over what is savvy. What is just over what is beneficial. What is God over what is man.

I promise that living this way will *lead* you straight to inner peace.

DAY 41

THE FIRST TIME

They say there's a first time for everything. But I think in everything, there should be a first-time mentality.

This year, I went to an Easter Vigil service at St. Francis of Assisi Church. I always enjoy seeing how excited new members are to be baptized, confirmed and receive the Eucharist for the first time. Things we often take for granted.

But what struck me was the passion of the more seasoned believers. Rather than just going through the motions, they were laughing, singing, dancing in the aisles, clapping, and cheering like newlyweds.

During the readings about Jesus's empty tomb, I even caught a couple people looking wide-eyed and joyful. Even though they have probably heard the Resurrection story hundreds of times, it was as if they were hearing it for the first time.

Rather than listening apathetically with their ears, they chose to listen enthusiastically with their hearts. The deep joy in their expressions encouraged me to take the same approach and nearly brought me to tears.

"Don't burn out; keep yourselves fueled and aflame. Be alert servants of the Master, cheerfully expectant. Don't quit in hard times; pray all the harder" (Romans 12:11 MSG).

All too often, the more familiar we get with the things and people in our lives, the more we become desensitized to their presence and significance. Whether it's a relationship, our faith, our careers, our friendships, our city, or just our day-to-day lives—they go from being new, exciting, and precious to old, common, and mundane.

But when we fully allow the Good News of the Easter story penetrate our hearts, a revival takes place. The more we are aware of our consistent shortcomings and the abundant love and mercy of God, we can't help but overflow with joy. Life and everything in it becomes a gift, not just a given.

As much as Easter is about Christ's resurrection, it is also about our own resurrection—dying to a life of selfishness and apathy and being reborn to a life of selflessness and love.

Imagine how drastically our lives would improve if we approached every event, relationship, and experience as if it was our first time:

Every morning you look at your wife, imagine you're just laying eyes on her for the first time at that restaurant. Every time you walk into class or rehearsal, imagine you just received that job or acceptance letter to the program of your dreams. Every day you walk through your city, act like you just moved there and can't help but pause and look up in awe at the incredible details around you.

Don't risk losing what you have to realize how much you have to lose. It's time to resuscitate every area of our lives, renew our vows, and plan second honeymoons.

Rather than just remembering and celebrating a resurrection that happened over two thousand years ago, may we allow Christ to resurrect our faith, relationships, callings, hearts, spirits, and lives *today*!

DAY 42

FREEDOM OF DISCIPLINE

I don't like the word *discipline*. It convicts me, makes me feel guilty, and wants to keep me from enjoying life. It tells me what I *can't* do and what I *can't* have, which just makes me want those things more.

For me, discipline only works when what I feel that I'm gaining more than I'm giving up.

Artists, for example, give up so many bodily and lifestyle comforts to pursue their crafts. Why? The feeling of ecstasy and aliveness we feel far outweigh any sacrifice.

When I stop dancing, I have less discipline because I forget all the benefits of eating well and staying fit. All I only focus on the discomfort of not being able to eat whatever I want and having to wake up early for the gym.

In order to make positive, lasting change, you *must* replace the pleasure of the old habits with an even more pleasurable habit. It's not enough to give up cake. You have to taste the endorphins from running.

Discipline then is not a way to keep you from enjoying life, but a way to enjoy life more. It is not about having less, but about keeping you from settling for less.

Let's indulge in discipline as a means of feasting on God.

DAY 43

TRUE HUMILITY

"Humility is not thinking less of yourself. It's thinking of yourself less" (C. S. Lewis).

Do you tend to put yourself down to others? Do you downplay your achievements to be humble and make sure others don't feel threatened?

I do.

What may seem humble, noble, and virtuous actually diminishes your power to positively impact another's life.

Whenever I'm playing small or holding back, I find I'm powerless to magnify anyone else or lift them up. All I can think about is myself and all my energy is directed inward.

But if I am thriving and full of life and feeling good about myself, I am able to get past my own needs and direct my energy outward.

Now don't get me wrong, I'm all for self-deprecating humor. (In fact, I think true confidence is being able to poke fun at yourself.) I'm also not condoning arrogance or bragging, which is just another way of expressing inequality from the other extreme.

I think we mistakenly assume there can only be one star at a time. Me or you. As if there were a limited amount of blessings or light so we better step up or move aside. That's why we feel the need to compare, compete, and envy.

But what if we considered there was an abundance of goodness and opportunity in this life—that your success in no way diminishes mine, and my success in no way diminishes yours.

True humility is not an exercise of division but one of multiplication. We were all made to shine in our own glorious ways, to light up this world together and make it the brightest it can possibly be.

Marianne Williamson said it best:

"Our deepest fear is not that we are inadequate. Our deepest fear is that we are powerful beyond measure. It is our light, not our darkness, that most frightens us. We ask ourselves, Who am I to be brilliant, gorgeous, talented, and fabulous? Actually, who are you not to be? You are a child of God. Your playing small does not serve the world. There is nothing enlightened about shrinking so that other people will not feel insecure around you. We are all meant to shine, as children do. We were born to make manifest the glory of God that is within us. It is not just in some of us; it is in everyone and as we let our own light shine, we unconsciously give others permission to do the same. As we are liberated from our own fear, our presence automatically liberates others."

*Side Note:

I'd also venture to say distorted humility may actually be a symptom of pride . . . assuming that what we have is ours to disparage, rather than God's gift to us.

Imagine your friend gives you a sweater, and another compliments that sweater. Would you say, "Oh, this ragged old thing?" No, because that would be offensive to the giver!

Similarly, when we realize all the talents and blessings we have are gifts from God, we do not diminish them in any way but rather point all the glory back to him.

So now when someone gives me a compliment, instead of rejecting it, I return it. That way we're both lifting each other in mutual celebration of God's abundant goodness.

DAY 44

GOD'S PEACE

It's a popular thing among believers to seek God's "peace" when making a decision. That's because we often confuse peace with comfort. I doubt most of the people in the Bible, Jesus included, had "peace" about what God was asking them to do. And they're still changing the world to this day.

For example, I recently returned from a mission trip in India through Promethean Spark where I taught kids in leprosy colonies life skills through dance.

It was one of the best and most rewarding decisions I have ever made. Yet, I felt a distinct lack of peace, even up until the second week I was there!

I wish I could tell you I jumped at the opportunity to go and trusted God wholeheartedly right from the beginning. After all, the year before, I quit my stable job to pursue the competitive world of dance, so I prided myself in being this huge risk taker.

But the reality is, I did *not* want to go to India (or was convinced I didn't). I was perfectly comfortable and content where I was, but deep down I knew something was missing. It just wouldn't leave me alone.

For months I barely slept, talked all my friends to death, exhausted Google, ate an obscene amount of peanut butter (as if the answer was at the bottom of the jar), cried to my then boyfriend, fasted, listened to sermons, agonized, kicked, and screamed.

I thought God would be angry with me for delaying. But God is patient . . . He uses those moments of doubt to grow our faith. Only a Father as brilliant as ours can master such irony. It gets our attention and gives Him the opportunity to intervene more powerfully in our lives.

One day I was walking to work, and a lady randomly stopped me on the street. She said, "Hello, I was just struck by your energy. My name is India, and I think you're meant to go to international. I see you rooting for the underdog."

What I felt at that moment wasn't peace. What I felt was God's presence saying, "Katie, do not be afraid. Come and follow me. I will bring you home. I love you, and you are mine" (David Haas).

God sent another angel to me in the form of a previous volunteer who also struggled with the decision. She provided me so much encouragement, patience and grace. Here is one of the quotes she sent me. I hope it helps you too:

"Nature loves courage. You make the commitment and nature will respond to that commitment by removing impossible obstacles. Dream the impossible dream and the world will not grind you under, it will lift you up. This is the trick. This is what all these teachers and philosophers who really counted, who really touched the alchemical gold, this is what they understood. This is the shamanic dance in the waterfall. This is how magic is done. By hurling yourself into the abyss and discovering it's a feather bed" (Terence McKenna).

When you are faced with a decision, consider for a moment the thing you don't want to do is actually the thing you did . . . if you only had all the information. God *does* have all the information. That's why we should trust Him with every decision.

***There's an incredible blog posting on this topic on *The Lipstick Gospel* blog, written by Stephanie May Wilson. I highly recommend all of her writings.

DAY 45

PUZZLE PIECES

Have you ever tried to change yourself to fit in? Maybe we should focus more on finding what fits us.

Growing up, I always felt a little off. I was very shy, self-conscious, and self-aware. I got nervous around people, never knew what to say in conversation, I wasn't interested in the same things as my peers, and just didn't seem to click.

All throughout high school and most of college, I wondered what was wrong with me. Maybe if I was more outgoing, skinny, funny, social, and talkative then I would finally feel accepted. And boy, did I try. Eventually, I began to accept the fact that things would probably never change and that I would feel like an outcast my whole life.

But senior year, I started meeting people through dance and church that I could relate to on many levels. My confidence, social skills, and relationship with God gradually started to build, and now seven years later, I am pursuing my dreams in New York City with a community of artists who inspire and encourage me to be *me* every day.

This week, I've had several conversations with dear friends who have or are still struggling with depression, anxiety, and feeling out of place. In case you did not watch the 2016 Oscars, here's what screenwriter Graham Moore has to say about that:

"When I was sixteen years old, I tried to kill myself because I felt weird and I felt different and I felt like I did not belong. And now I'm standing here. So I would like for this moment to be for that kid out there who feels like she's weird or she's different or she doesn't fit in anywhere. Yes, you do. I promise you do. Stay weird, stay different, and then when it's your turn and you are standing on this stage, please pass the same message on to the next person who comes along."

Even God doesn't require you to fit into some Christian mold. In fact, quite the opposite. You were created to fit perfectly into God's grand design. If you change just one piece of a puzzle, it cannot be completed. So don't! You just need to find the right surrounding pieces.

DAY 46

SETTING BOUNDARIES

Two types of boundaries are needed in this industry—time and ethics.

Time . . .

When I first started in this industry, I said yes to everything. I attended every class, audition, rehearsal, workshop, seminar, work-study, and volunteer opportunity I could . . . on top of working to pay the bills.

Before long, my desire to succeed began to diminish. I was stretched thin, exhausted, undernourished, and after a while, uninspired.

We tend to think that saying "no" or turning down and opportunity or sitting out a class admits defeat or weakness. In fact, it's the complete opposite. We need boundaries to stay strong.

Yesterday, I had about fifty things going on: two job interviews, rehearsal, class, errands, and social commitments . . . but I planned to wedge in a theater class from my favorite teacher in between. I had twenty minutes to run to my apartment, change, get on the subway and run to the studio. Déjà vu. I even called ahead to make sure the class was still open.

I barely got out the door when I realized how stressed out and frantic I was becoming because of this decision. I pondered, what if I sat this one out, got all my things done, and then was able to enjoy the party tonight. It's always hard for me to make "logical" choices like that because I don't want to miss out. But I decided to experiment.

During the time I would have been in class, I was able to have an important conversation with my dad, have a phone interview with my future employer, respond to all my emails, and calmly get ready to leave. It was a real blessing and really changed my mood the rest of the day. Success!

This same principle applies to our relationships. As artists, we have such big hearts that we open up to everything and everyone around us . . . but we rarely filter out what comes in. This makes us susceptible to getting burned out, discouraged, and taken advantage of. We need to set boundaries early on in our relationships so that they enable our success and not hinder it.

Ethics . . .

Have you ever been to an audition that made you feel uneasy? Or a role you didn't really feel good about playing but did it anyway to make money?

There is a *huge* temptation to sell your soul for the sake of work, recognition, and success . . . especially in a field where doors don't open every day.

As performers, we're always told to honor that inner voice and go with our gut in every little choice we make, so shouldn't that apply to our career as a whole? Just because performers are called to be a blank slate, that does not give anyone the right to come over and scribble on us.

Start being very intentional about what you want your brand to be and what you want your career to say.

If you have an agent, be very clear about what roles you feel comfortable playing. If you're ever uncomfortable at an audition, discreetly tell the supervisor you have another appointment and excuse yourself from the room.

This may seem like surefire ways to slow your progress, but I firmly believe that betraying yourself will only lessen your legacy because it diminishes the essence of *you* and what people receive from your work.

Do not prostitute your gifts. Hold out for the opportunities that makes them shine in all their glory.

DAY 47

OPINIONS

"The bad stuff is easier to believe. You ever notice that?" *(Pretty Woman)*

This is especially true in our subjective, competitive, and demanding industry. No matter how much encouragement we get, one negative comment can really set us back and make us question it all.

The saddest part is these comments usually come from the people we trust most: well-meaning friends, parents, mentors, teachers, significant others, etc. So we tend to believe them more.

The other day in ballet, my teacher looked at me and said, "If you can't hold a passé, you should either be in a different class or a different profession."

My neighbor's voice teacher said, "You will never be a pop singer because you will only be cast in classical, legit roles."

My friend's mentor told her, "If you haven't made it in the business by your age, you probably never will."

I wonder how many people's dreams have suffered a premature death because they accepted one negative opinion as a fact. We must remember that just because someone says it, that doesn't make it true.

Fred Astaire—told by the *Chicago Tribune*, "Can't act. Can't sing. Balding. Can dance a little."

Elvis Presley—told by his manager, "You ain't goin' nowhere, son. You ought to go back to drivin' a truck."

Thomas Edison—teachers told him he was "too stupid to learn anything."

Sidney Poitier—told by a casting director, "Why don't you stop wasting people's time and go out and become a dishwasher or something?"

Oprah—first boss told her she was "too emotional and not right for television."

Beatles—rejected by Decca Records who said, "We don't like their sound, and guitar music is on the way out."

Walt Disney—fired from a Missouri newspaper at age twenty-two for "not being creative enough."

Stop replaying the opinions of small-minded men, and replace them the promises of an all-powerful God. Only His opinions are also facts.

> "Jesus looked at them intently and said, 'Humanly speaking, it is impossible. But with God everything is possible'" (Matthew 19:26 NLT).

> "For I know the plans I have for you," declares the LORD, "plans to prosper you and not to harm you, plans to give you hope and a future" (Jeremiah 29:11 NIV).

> "Commit to the Lord whatever you do, and your plans will succeed" (Proverbs 16:3 NLT).

> "I can do all things through Christ who strengthens me" (Philippians 4:13 NKJV).

Enough said. Literally.

DAY 48

JUDGMENT

I have a fear of being judged.

Before a voice lesson, I ask my teacher not to judge me. Before an advanced class, I ask my friends to not judge me. Before sharing my thoughts in a meeting, I ask my co-workers not to judge me.

I want everyone to like me, assume I'm super talented, like all my ideas, and agree with everything I say. I would rather hide under the pretty mask of perfection than reveal the fact that I'm flawed and a fraud.

When it comes to being judged, the real problem isn't other people. It's our own *pride*, which not only helps us save face, but condemns us to a life of mediocrity.

For example, I've been putting off taking ballet for the past year because I'm afraid people will notice my technique is slipping and I'm out of shape. What happens as a result? My technique slips more, and I get more out of shape.

A couple weeks ago, I got up the courage to go to class and planned to remain anonymous in the back. Just then a friend of mine came in the room, and my first instincts were to either hide or try really hard to impress him.

But then I decided to laugh it off, do my best, and just accept where I'm at. I was clearly the inferior dancer. When I complimented him after class, he looked shocked and said that he was really self-conscious because he was having an off day. He was just as worried about me judging him.

There's a quote that says, in your twenties you care what others think about you, in your thirties you don't care what others think about you, and in your forties you realize no one was ever really thinking about you. They were thinking about themselves.

The truth is, the only judgment we should fear is God's. Because then we're confident enough to not need it from others and humble enough to keep ourselves in check according to His standards.

> "Do not think of yourself more highly than you ought, but rather think of yourself with sober judgment, in accordance with the faith God has distributed to each of you" (Romans 12:3 NIV).

> "In the fear of the LORD there is strong confidence, And his children will have refuge" (Proverbs 14:26 KJV).

> "Before a downfall the heart is haughty, but humility comes before honor" (Proverbs 18:12 NIV).

> "Stop regarding man, whose breath of life is in his nostrils; for why should he be esteemed" (Isaiah 2:22 NASB)?

> "Have I not commanded you? Be strong and courageous! Do not tremble or be dismayed, for the LORD your God is with you wherever you go" (Joshua 1:9 NIV).

DAY 49

SLOTH

Laziness is not usually a term we associate with artists. Quite the opposite, in fact. After all, it's easy to work hard at something you're passionate about.

But what about the other things in our lives entrusted to us: our day jobs, our families, our relationships. Are we just doing the bare minimum to get by?

Pastor Kerrick Thomas says there's a lot of talk in this city about "following" our passion, but that instead we should "bring" our passion into every area of life.

I remember being very convicted by this last year when another girl my age started working at my company. She was always so bubbly, friendly, enthusiastic, and just a ray of sunshine. This was not her dream job. But she decided to bring her joy into the job, rather than depending on the job to bring her joy.

Meanwhile, all I could think of was that I didn't want to be there because I just wanted to be dancing. This attitude led to frustration, then complacency, and eventually a lack of drive to pursue much of anything. When we let apathy take over one area of our lives, it inevitably infects the others.

(I didn't see at the time, but this job would allow me to save enough money to teach dance in India and would be right there waiting for me when I got back to continue financing my dance career.)

God doesn't make mistakes. He brings all the right people and opportunities into our lives for a reason, even if we don't realize it. With that in mind, how could we not give everything we have to everything we have, knowing that God is using it for our benefit?

Sometimes, we assume that following God means living a boring, obedient life. But God *created* all the fascinating, interesting things in the world we're so passionate about. He is the ultimate Dreamer, Dramatist and Thrill-seeker! He wants to show you His dreams for you are *much bigger* than your own.

Treat every menial job, unpaid project, and acquaintance as a milestone on your journey and not a detour. When we give God the ordinary, He gives us the *extraordinary*. May we remain diligent and pass the test.

> "If you are faithful in little things, you will be faithful in large ones. But if you are dishonest in little things, you won't be honest with greater responsibilities" (Luke 16:10 NLT).

> "Work hard and cheerfully at whatever you do, as though you were working for the Lord rather than for people" (Colossians 3:23 NLT).

Remember, when you put God first, life is *one big adventure*!

DAY 50

SURRENDER

As artists, we *try so hard*. We rush from classes to auditions to work study to our day jobs, all the while feeling guilty for not fitting in the gym. We try to impress our teachers in class, casting directors in auditions, and our peers with our accomplishments.

It's exhausting!

We fear if we don't do these things, we'll never accomplish our dreams. But this frantic, control-freak approach often has the opposite effect—the more we try to control things, the more out of control they get.

In his book *The Me I Want to Be*, John Ortberg says the key to getting the desires of our hearts is to surrender.

Usually when we hear the word surrender, we immediately think of defeat. It's what people do when they give up or lose hope. But when it comes to God, surrender means victory. It's the only way to win.

My friend put it this way . . . imagine you're standing a pool of water. You keep frantically moving around, trying desperately to see your reflection, but the waves and ripples obstruct your vision.

Only when you stand still and let the waters settle can you finally see things clearly.

I had a really hard time surrendering to God's will to go to India. I didn't see how that fit in at all with my plans or would help further my career. But when I finally decided to follow God's plan instead of my own, I gained more training, dance experience, contacts, and lifelong friends than I ever would have otherwise.

That whole experience was God's way of saying, "Katie, trust me. I know what I'm doing."

I encourage you to let God be your agent. Just as you would trust Bloch or MSA with your career, try trusting the Author of your destiny—the One who knows every person in the business, every show, every opportunity, and has the power to get your foot in any door.

With God, you *always* get out more than you put in. Your own dreams are just scratching the surface.

> "I tell you the truth, unless a kernel of wheat falls to the ground and dies, it remains only a single seed. But if it dies, it produces many seeds" (John 12:24 NLT).

DAY 51

DESIRE

Sometimes, I think God doesn't like me unless I'm doing *spiritual* things like praying or listening to a sermon. As if He's somewhat displeased when I get joy from anything else I desire besides Him like dance, food, music, movies, etc.

This perception pegs God as a possessive killjoy that only gets pleasure when we give up pleasure. It's what causes us to burn out and lose our interest in spirituality and passion for God.

As John Ortberg says, "Nothing makes a human being more vulnerable to temptation than a joyless life."

God is not threatened by our joy, but delights when we delight in something He created. If you gave your child a gift, would you not get immense pleasure from seeing them come alive every time they played with it?

Instead of trying to force joy into some isolated relationship with God, try putting Him at the center of everything you enjoy. Instead of leaving God out of "nonspiritual" activities, make him the center of everything, *especially* your passions. These are His greatest gifts.

"Every good and perfect gift comes from above, from the Father of all lights who satisfies the desires of those who fear him" (James 1:17 NIV).

We need to learn to associate the two: God and joy. The gift and the Giver. In fact, it's when we do separate the two, that our passions become idols. Nothing good should be separate from God because everything good is *from* God. He doesn't want you to give up the gift. He wants you to lift up the Giver.

"God is so great that he does not need to be our only joy. There is an earthly joy, a joy of the outer as well as the inner self, the joy of dancing as well as kneeling, the joy of playing as well as praying" (Lewis Smedes).

God never commanded us to *only* find joy in Him, but that we keep Him at the center of our joy.

Here are practical steps from Ortberg:

— Take a moment at the beginning of the day to invite God to be with you.
— Consciously say "thank you" to Him in the midst of your enjoyment.
— Meet other people who share your joys, so that you add community to your delight.
— Put pictures on your screensaver that remind you of God's goodness.
— Use a "breath prayer" like "thank you for my body" or "taste and see."
— Reflect on Psalm 103.

DAY 52

LIP SERVICE

Lip service does not count as service.

It's one thing for me to sit on my comfy bed and write truths, but it's another thing for me to put down my teddy and live them out.

One particular incident convicted me. I had an interview where I had to list the world causes I care about. One of the things I said was "feeding the hungry and homeless." I left the interview feeling all warm and fuzzy.

On my way out, I received a text from my friend asking if I could come to an event tonight for Catholic Charities where we feed the homeless in NYC. Enter, feelings less warm, less fuzzy.

I had been sitting in the office all day, looking forward to my ballet and hip-hop classes this evening. In the big picture, which was more important—that I take class or that my actions were consistent with my words?

Knowing the right decision, I immediately texted her back, Yes. (So I wouldn't change my mind.)

It's true, sometimes it's also OK say no. You can serve wherever you are in ways that aren't so blatantly philanthropic. But I've also experienced that putting God's plans ahead of my own leads to immeasurable blessings.

Tonight was no exception. I met so many wonderful people my age and was able to enjoy a long walk home with God in this glorious weather, listening to music.

On the way, I stopped to hand a handicapped, homeless man one of the sack lunches we prepared. He absolutely lit up, kissed my hand and called me lovely. A passing of the Spirit from one soul to another.

Life took on a whole different meaning for me tonight, far beyond any class, dream or passion the world has to offer. The gift of simply being able to live, serve, and share this beautiful world with others—*that* is truly a life worth living.

May all of us who rush, clutch, grasp, toil, sweat, reach, search, and struggle to make it in this business realize that everything we truly need to be fulfilled is all around us. Have the courage to unclench your fists, and you'll be surprised at how much more you'll be able to receive.

I thought I was going to be feeding people tonight. I didn't realize they would be feeding me.

DAY 53

BUSY

We brag about being busy like it's a badge of honor. The busier we are, the more productive and important we think we are. "Just keeping busy" has become a widely acceptable social response.

I am by far the biggest offender of this. I have my entire schedule planned to the minute. I leave little room to breathe, let alone for the Spirit.

Yesterday, I rushed from my job to an appointment to happy hour to the store to a service event to meet a friend to call my mom and watch a movie. I have become the girl who stops by and leaves early, on to her next "important person" duty.

Here's the truth: busyness is the number one barrier to spiritual growth and relationships. Why? Because both require something busy people don't have—*time*.

> "If you don't have time to pray and read the Scriptures, you are busier than God ever intended you to be" (Matthew Kelly).

We spread ourselves so thin, our relationships with God and others lack any depth. Anything of substance cannot be forced or rushed, but must develop slowly and steadily over time. We try to fill the void by piling on more activities, which only deepens the void.

As Pastor Doug Fields of Saddleback Church explains, "If we're moving too fast, we're no longer *following* Jesus, we're trying to *lead* Him. Our Savior is one who *walks*, not runs. If we are to walk with Him, we need to slow our pace."

The best way to do this is to exercise your *no* muscle. *No*, you are not the Savior of the world. *No*, you are not the only person capable of filling a certain role. *No*, you are not supposed to say yes to every good thing that comes your way.

Actually, when we say *yes* to every opportunity, we are saying *no* to God's best for us. In fact, busyness is the number one way Satan keeps us distracted and unproductive. He knows God can often use us more when our schedules are open.

So stop trying to please everyone and be all things to all people. Stop trying to impress others with how spiritual and involved you are. Start guarding your schedule so God can fill it with His agenda.

Then enjoy the peace of mind, rejuvenation, and ease that comes from living your life the way you were intended to.

DAY 54

GIVING UP

It's not a matter of *if* we give up, but *what* we give up.

I used to think moving away from my Broadway pursuits would qualify me as a failure. I would have to live the rest of my life knowing I gave up on my dreams.

But then I realized, whether I pursue my dreams or not, I will inevitably be giving up something. This changes how I view success and failure.

Do I give up my career in advertising, my relationship, living close to my family, financial stability, the ability to support my family? Or do I want to give up the chance to be on stage, live in New York, and pursue my passion?

The movie, *Whiplash*, is an excellent demonstration of this inner conflict and the consequences that result. The main character chooses to give up his relationship, family harmony, physical comfort, and emotional sanity to avoid giving up on his dreams.

He is told by his abusive teacher that becoming one of the "greats" means persisting at all costs—even to the point of self-destruction. Another student who buys into this philosophy ends up hanging himself because he becomes consumed by the pursuit and depression.

Let's get one thing clear . . . God gave you gifts and passions to bring you and others closer to Him. He did *not* give you gifts and passions for your own ego, fame, or superiority. Our gifts were intended to enhance our lives and the world around us, *not* to help us self-destruct or lead others into sin.

This is called abusing our gifts, and we have *all* been guilty of it, especially in this city. Satan loves to take the joy we get from our passions and pervert it with pride, greed, and fame. God uses our gifts to *create*. Satan uses our gifts to *destroy*.

Artists, do not fall for this tempting scheme!

The choice to give up your plans for God's plans is *never* an act of defeat. Sometimes they will be the same, and sometimes they will be different. But they will *always* lead to our most glorious and victorious life.

Rick Warren uses the story of Moses to make this point: God asked Moses to set down his shepherd staff, aka his livelihood. When Moses did, God turned the staff into a miracle-performing tool, which would eventually lead the Egyptians out of captivity.

In other words, when we set down what we have, God gives us more than we could ever imagine.

Jesus did not simply "give up" on the cross. He gave up His life so that we wouldn't have to give up our eternity. He gave up His will for the Father's. His was the ultimate example of giving up something good for something greater.

What is God asking you to give up in your life? I promise you, it's a trade worth making.

DAY 55

TEMPTATION

We all have an area of our life that we struggle with. Mine is food.

Whenever I am bored, anxious, or just want to avoid my feelings, I turn to food for comfort. Snacking is the default setting of my brain when my mind is idle.

Many of us think that overcoming temptation is simply a matter of discipline or willpower. But as John Ortberg says, "The will is easily fatigued." Approaching habits through of self-denial is only a temporary fix.

The solution is not have *more* willpower; the solution is having *less* of our own will involve and more of the Father's.

Pastor Rick Warren says not to resist temptation because what we resist, persists. He says that we should rather *replace* the temptation or habit with a positive activity. That way, instead of denying ourselves pleasure, we rewire our brains to seek pleasure elsewhere. Thus, the temptation loses its power.

Temptations are not only *attractions*, they are *distractions*—keeping our minds disproportionately focused on one thing, while we miss out on life's greater blessings.

John Ortberg says our biggest sins are tied with our biggest strengths. The very qualities that help us thrive in one area lead to our downfall in another.

For example, I have a huge appetite for life. When I'm dancing, I go full out, perform big, get a surge of energy, hoot and holler, and wave my hair around. I go crazy. The same is also true in less healthy areas of my life—like overeating and overworking.

Instead of allowing your temptations to remind you of your weaknesses, let them remind you of your strengths. Negativity leads to more of the same negative results. Positivity leads to positive change.

Pastor Rick Muchow from Saddleback Church sees temptation as an opportunity to worship. We typically reduce worship to singing in church on Sundays. But says every time we chose to turn from the temptation to God, it is an act of spiritual worship. Your battlefield could become your ultimate platform of praise.

> "Finally, brothers and sisters, whatever is true, whatever is noble, whatever is right, whatever is pure, whatever is lovely, whatever is admirable— if anything is excellent or praiseworthy—think about such things" (Philippians 4:8 NIV).

DAY 56

BECOMING

Many of our dreams revolve around two things: career and relationship.

We focus so much on *finding* the right job or the right person, when we should be focusing on *becoming* that person.

Ask yourself the following questions:

— Would I hire myself in my dream job? (Consider work ethic, discipline, drive, talents, enthusiasm, knowledge, experience, etc.)

— Would I ask me to marry me? (Consider character, habits, temper, priorities, relationship skills, selflessness, etc.)

Often times, I get frustrated when my dreams haven't happened or I haven't met the right person yet. We can pray and dream all we want, but if we aren't doing our part to develop ourselves, God is not going magically decide to entrust them to us.

Many times we attract the things we want in life, not by seeking them out, but by becoming the one the person or job we're looking for is looking for.

While this is certainly convicting, it is also very empowering. It means there is actually something we can be doing to work toward our dreams, rather than just sitting around helpless and frustrated.

That's why it's so important that we are constantly seeking to improve ourselves. We need to prepare ourselves spiritually by staying tuned into God, emotionally by learning how to nurture healthy relationships, and physically by being in class. In that order.

God would rather withhold your dreams until you're ready than put you in a situation you cannot handle. He wants to give you the type of career and person you desire. But first, He wants to help you qualify for the position.

> "Do you not know that in a race all the runners run, but only one receives the prize? So run that you may obtain it. Every athlete exercises self-control in all things. They do it to receive a perishable wreath, but we an imperishable. So I do not run aimlessly; I do not box as one beating the air. But I discipline my body and keep it under control, lest after preaching to others I myself should be disqualified" (1 Corinthians 9:24–27 ESV).

> "All Scripture is breathed out by God and profitable for teaching, for reproof, for correction, and for training in righteousness, that the man of God may be competent, equipped for every good work" (2 Timothy 3:16–17 NASB).

> "I appeal to you therefore, brothers, by the mercies of God, to present your bodies as a living sacrifice, holy and acceptable to God, which is your spiritual worship. Do not be conformed to this world, but be transformed by the renewal of your mind, that by testing you may discern what

is the will of God, what is good and acceptable and perfect" (Romans 12:1–2 NIV).

"Do not be slothful in zeal, be fervent in spirit, serve the Lord" (Romans 12:11 ESV).

DAY 57

EMBRACING PAIN

Pain gets our attention.

Sometimes it's easy for us to sin because we don't see the consequences right away. In a sense, it feels as if we get away with it, so there is no incentive to change.

But there inevitably comes a time when we hit rock bottom—we feel the full weight of our decisions, and everything is exposed. Often times the pain and shame of going through an experience like this is a wake-up call and turning point in our lives. It is God's way of getting our attention.

> "Pain insists upon being attended to. God whispers to us in our pleasures, speaks in our consciences, but shouts in our pains. It is his megaphone to rouse a deaf world" (C. S. Lewis).

Imagine you have a dull pain in your foot and don't do anything about it. It's going to keep getting worse and worse. Eventually, you will start to develop a limp, and people will notice the toll it's taking on your life. Then the day will come when you can no longer walk on it, and you are forced to go to the doctor.

This is usually the approach we take with sin in our lives. We wait and go to God when we have no other choice, rather than making him our first choice when we feel that first dull ache.

I've been struggling with bad eating habits lately, but I've only experienced minor discomforts. Until this morning. I must have eaten something bad last night when snacking because I've had food poisoning all day. I had to leave work early, miss out on class, and nearly went to the emergency room.

As miserable as I was, I couldn't help but thank God for shaking me up and giving me an incentive to change my behavior. No pain, no change.

***Also be cognizant to the pain of others around you. In this busy city, I have cried in public many times—on the subway and on the street—and people don't seem to notice. Lend a listening ear or a comforting smile, and be willing to talk about your struggles. God could use your pain as another person's hope.

Where do you need a wake-up call? What area of your life do you feel a dull ache? I urge you to shout out to God for help before he has to shout out to you.

> "I will not cause pain without allowing something new to be born, says the Lord" (Isaiah 66:9 NCV).

> "Yet what we suffer now is nothing compared to the glory he will reveal to us later" (Romans 8:18 NLT).

DAY 58

MAKING DECISIONS

I don't know about you, but I have a hard time making decisions. Let's just say, I'm never someone you want to go shopping with.

Whenever I face a crossroads in my life, I agonize over it and exhaust all the pros and cons. I ask advice, read books, listen to sermons, pray, fast, and anything else I can think of right up until the deadline.

When I was deciding whether or not to go to India, I struggled a lot. I felt guilty for not saying "yes" right away. You hear about people in the Bible who left their livelihoods to obey God or follow Jesus at the drop of a hat. Was my lack of peace from inner fear or God interfering?

I kept repeating the same self-condemning phrase that delayed obedience is disobedience. These feelings were entirely self-inflicted and a product of my own misguided conscience, fears, confusion. Even the founder of the program was incredibly patient and encouraged me to pray and wait for God's peace.

Tonight, I heard a sermon by Pastor Rick Warren that made me think differently about decision-making. He said whenever we are feeling pressured to make a decision, that pressure is not from God.

Our God is a patient God who values careful discernment, consideration and planning, not hasty judgments based on our hunches or feelings.

> "The plans of the diligent lead surely to advantage, But everyone who is hasty comes surely to poverty" (Proverbs 21:5 NASB).

> "Also it is not good for a person to be without knowledge, And he who hurries his footsteps errs" (Proverbs 19:2 NASB).

Rick suggests before your next decision, go through these steps he calls Solomon's Eight Steps of Wisdom:

1. Check the Bible (every answer you need is in there)
2. Get the facts (research, determine the need)
3. Ask for advice (from people who have made a similar decision)
4. Set a faith goal (dreams become more attainable with a deadline)
5. Calculate the cost (time, money, energy, effect on family/ relationships)
6. Plan for problems (they will come)
7. Face your fears (courage and fear go together)
8. Step out in faith (trust God's promises over your fears)

Sometimes when I really don't know what to do, I'll pray this simple prayer: *Lord, please close all the wrong doors and open all the right doors. I'm really making a mess of things here, and I need you to intervene.*

> No matter what decision you make, decide to "entrust your work to the LORD, and your planning will succeed" (Proverbs 16:3 NLT).

DAY 59

FINDING JOY

Sometimes we let the discipline, technique, and hard work of our craft take away from the joy of it.

I'm especially reminded of this in ballet. It's entirely possible to make it through an entire hour and a half of ballet without so much as cracking a smile. Because ballet is so challenging and precise, we forget it is also a form of dancing and deserves as much joy and passion as any other.

In ballet the other day, instead of being stiff and striving to be perfect, I focused on fullness of movement, letting my arms soar and face shine expressively. The class went from being a drudgery to a pleasurable experience.

I am always drawn to the older women in class who aren't polished or perfect by any means, but are incredibly happy to be there. They are less self-conscious and more willing to let go and have fun and live. Watching them does much more for my spirit than the most beautiful dancer in the room.

In fact, every instance of dance mentioned in the Bible involves some expression of joy. Here are a few:

"A time to cry and a time to laugh. A time to grieve and a time to dance" (Ecclesiastes 3:4 NLT).

"You have turned for me my mourning into dancing: you have put off my sackcloth, and girded me with gladness" (Psalms 30:11 AKJV).

"Let them praise his name in the dance: let them sing praises to him with the tambourine and harp" (Psalms 149:3 NASB).

My good friend said she is naturally drawn to the dance forms that make the Spirit come alive in her. Cultures all around the world use dance to express joy and gratitude:

Bhangra (Punjab, India) —danced by workers in a field to life their spirits, celebrates the harvest, weddings.

West African—celebrates a birth, harvest or death, wards off evil spirits, to ask the gods for prosperity, or to resolve conflict.

Flamenco—performed at weddings and Spanish celebrations, "having soul, a heightened state of emotion, expression and authenticity."

Whatever feeling is being evoked through your art, make sure the inner intensity and intention match the physicality of it. Otherwise, art becomes just another spectator sport, instead of a transformative, participatory experience.

The same applies to your spiritual life or anything else you do. Robotic living doesn't do much for you and certainly doesn't impact others.

Never just go through the motions. Go through the emotions. And bring others along for the ride.

DAY 60

APPRECIATION

As the glam metal band, Cinderella, says, "You don't know what you got till it's gone."

We don't appreciate what we have until we lose it. This is a sad reality of the human condition to take what we have for granted. We tend to focus on the negatives of things we have and the positives of things we don't have. We exist in a perpetual state of lack. It's a really bad habit.

When I am in a relationship, I worry about my career. When I'm content with my career, I worry about my relationship. It's like I am unable to see what the right decision is until I make the wrong decision. It's a real problem, and it's caused me to hurt my relationships, career, and inner sense of peace.

Every night before I go to bed, I make a list of things I'm grateful for that day. I begin the list with "Lord, thank You for this day!" Then I list everything from a smile on the subway to a new job opportunity. It makes me cognizant of so many blessings that I would otherwise overlook. It's amazing how many God can pack into one day!

Today, I decided to do that same exercise in a more specific, intentional way. On a piece of paper I made a column for every major aspect of my life (dance studio, marketing job, apartment, church, relationship, and New York City) and wrote down all the benefits of each one. Rather than focusing on the cons, I'm training my brain to focus on the pros. This helps me to see each one as a gift from God along my journey instead of a burden.

Most of us spend our prayer time making more requests. But at any given moment, we are living in the middle of an answered prayer. Instead of focusing on what you want to ask for in the future, give thanks for what you asked for in the past are able to enjoy in the present.

The best part about giving someone a gift is the appreciation they show you. The same is true of God. The more gratitude we show, the more pleasure He gets from giving us more.

> As my mentor says, "Delight yourself in the Lord, and He will give you the desires of your heart" (Psalm 37:4 ESV).

> "Give thanks in all circumstances; for this is the will of God in Christ Jesus for you" (1 Thessalonians 5:18 ESV).

> "And whatever you do, in word or deed, do everything in the name of the Lord Jesus, giving thanks to God the Father through him" (Colossians 3:17).

> "This is the day the Lord has made. Let us rejoice and be glad" (Psalm 118:24 ESV).

Lord, thank You for this day!

ABOUT THE AUTHOR

Katie Homer is a working copywriter and dancer living in New York City. She currently teaches Bollywood at Steps on Broadway, tours internationally with AATMA Performing Arts, and recently costarred as Liza Minnelli in a musical production called Hats Off to Liza. Katie is also the founder of an arts-based ministry called GODWAY (http://tinyurl.com/lx4pw22)—from which these devotionals originated—that encourages and educates artists on how to thrive in the industry with integrity. She is eternally grateful to God, the source of *everything* good in her life, and resolves to live each day pointing the glory back to Him.

CPSIA information can be obtained
at www.ICGtesting.com
Printed in the USA
BVHW07s0951121018
529912BV00002B/788/P